Class No.	Book No.
371.914	05983

Author
ELLIS, Andrew W.

Title   Reading, writing and dyslexia: A cognitive analysis.
2nd ed.

Reading, Writing and Dyslexia
A Cognitive Analysis

Andrew W. Ellis
Department of Psychology
University of York
York, UK

Second Edition

 **Psychology Press**
Taylor & Francis Group

HOVE AND NEW YORK

Published in 1993 by Psychology Press Ltd
27 Church Road, Hove, East Sussex, BN3 2FA

www.psypress.co.uk

Psychology Press is part of the Taylor & Francis Group

Reprinted in paperback 1994, 1995, 1998, 2001 and 2003

British Library Cataloguing in Publication Data
A catalogue record for this book is available from the British Library

ISBN 0-86377-307-9

Printed and bound in the UK by TJ International Ltd, Padstow, Cornwall

For my mother and father

Contents

Preface to the Second Edition

When I was first asked to produce a second edition of this book, I imagined that it would be a relatively simple matter of changing or inserting the odd phrase or reference and improving the wording here and there. When I sat down to it, however, I realised that it was not going to be that easy. The study of reading, writing and dyslexia has advanced so much in the last 10 years that it has proven necessary to start again and effectively write a fresh book. Fragments of the old have survived here and there (notably in the first chapter which deals with the origins, evolution and nature of writing), but this is largely a new book. In a sense, that is a shame because a lot of people seemed to like the first edition. I can only hope that this new version does not disappoint.

I have retained the broad organisation of the first edition. The book opens with a consideration of the history and nature of writing in Chapter 1, then moves on to three chapters dealing with the nature of skilled reading (word recognition in Chapters 2 and 3, text processing in Chapter 4). Chapter 5 is concerned with the different ways that brain injury in adulthood can disrupt the mature reading skill; that is, with the "acquired dyslexias". Chapter 6 considers spelling and writing processes, both in skilled writers and in patients with "acquired dysgraphia". Only in Chapter 7 do we consider the learning process—how children develop the skills of reading and writing. One of the changes here in comparison with the first edition is a more thorough treatment of the teaching of reading. Chapter 8 deals with developmental reading and writing problems. This is a book about reading *and* writing and *both* forms of dyslexia—acquired and developmental: it is not a book that is exclusively (or even primarily) concerned with developmental dyslexia.

As in the first edition, I have tried to write a book which is accessible to a non-psychologist but which might also be used as part of an undergraduate psychology course. The production of this second edition coincided with a term of office as Head of the Department of Psychology at the University of York. I would not recommend that combination to anyone. It has, however, helped enormously to have been working in a department where so many people are studying aspects of the reading process. People at York who have contributed to the development of the ideas presented here include (in strictly alphabetical order) Sue Franklin, Evi Graf, Peter Hatcher, Kathi Hirsh, Charles Hulme, Siné McDougall, Andrew Monk, Catriona Morrison, John Rack and Sue Stothard. My thanks to all of them. Once again, Anna, Martin and Hayden have provided sympathy, encouragement and the right amount of distraction.

Andrew W. Ellis
York, December 1992

Preface to the First Edition

Reading and writing have been the objects of intensive psychological research in recent years. Much of this work has focused on the skilled reader and writer, but there have been other valuable and interesting approaches. One of these has been the analysis of how brain injury can impair reading and writing in previously literate adults--the study, that is, of the acquired dyslexias and dysgraphias. Developmental problems in learning to read and write have also been investigated by cognitive psychologists, as has the acquisition of literacy by normal children. It is my personal belief that real advances are being made on all these fronts, and this book is an attempt to summarize and convey those advances. The book is aimed primarily at students of psychology or education, but I have tried at the same time to make the book intelligible to parents, teachers, and anyone else coming afresh to the investigation of reading, writing, and dyslexia. In addition, the book contains accounts of much recent or unpublished research, and also some of my own ideas. I hope that on these grounds it will also interest professionals in the field. Two people have had a particularly strong influence on the development of my own thinking about reading, writing, and dyslexia. They are John Marshall and John Morton, and I should like to take this opportunity to thank them publicly. I have been fortunate enough to have worked for the past five years at Lancaster University. I should like to thank all my colleagues for creating such a friendly and stimulating atmosphere, but I have benefited particularly from exchanges of ideas with Alan Collins, Lesley Galpin,

Dennis Hay, Phil Levy, Diane Miller, Peter Morris, Mary Smyth, and, last only on alphabetic grounds, Andy Young. If this book has any merit whatsoever it is due in no small measure to the extremely helpful comments on earlier drafts received from Max Coltheart, Karalyn Patterson, Leslie Henderson, Alan Collins, Tim Miles, and Maggie Snowling. I only wish I could have answered satisfactorily all of the points they raised. Alan Collins prepared the indices, Anne Parker, Sylvia Sumner, and Hazel Satterthwaite typed various portions of various drafts, and Anne Jackson drew the figures. My thanks to them. The writing of this book was facilitated by grants HR 7485 and CO 023-2042 from the Social Science Research Council. Finally I should like to thank Anna for everything, and Martin and Hayden for helping me maintain a sense of proportion.

Andrew W. Ellis
Lancaster, April 1983

CHAPTER ONE

Written Language

THE ORIGINS OF WRITING

Prehistoric people used pictures to convey information, as did (or do) several more recent cultures without writing systems in North America, Central Africa, Southeastern Asia and Siberia. Figure 1.1 shows a rock drawing found near a precipitous trail in New Mexico. It warns the "reader" that, while a mountain goat (with horns) may hope to pass safely, a rider on horseback is certain to fall. "Picture writing" of this sort may be quite sophisticated in what it conveys. Figure 1.2 shows a drawing found on the face of a rock on the shore of Lake Superior in Michigan and relates the course of an Indian military expedition. The meaning of the drawing is provided by Gelb (1963, pp. 29–30). The five canoes at the top carry 51 men, represented by the vertical strokes. A chieftain called Kishkemunasee, "Kingfisher", leads the expedition. He is represented by the bird drawn above the first canoe. The three suns under three arches show that the journey lasted 3 days. The turtle symbolises a happy landing, and the picture of a man on a horse shows that the warriors marched on quickly. The courageous spirit of the warriors is captured in the drawing of the eagle, while force and cunning are evoked in the symbols of the panther and serpent.

The interpretation of Fig. 1.2 is by no means self-evident: one needs to be a member of the culture to know, for example, that a turtle can symbolise a happy landing. Note, though, that there is no single, correct way to "read"

FIG. 1.1. Indian rock drawing from New Mexico (from G. Mallery, *Picture-writing of the American Indians*. Tenth Annual Report of the Bureau of Ethology, Smithsonian Institution, Washington, 1893).

FIG. 1.2. Indian rock drawing from Michigan (from H. R. Schoolcraft, *Historical and Statistical Information, Respecting the History, Condition, and Prospects of the Indian Tribes of the United States*, Part 1, Philadelphia, 1851).

Fig. 1.2: its meaning may be expressed many ways in English and no doubt in equally many ways in the language of the Native American who drew it. Picture writing differs from true writing in this respect— there are many ways to "read" a picture (that is, to convert its message into words), but only one way to read a sentence.

THE EMERGENCE OF TRUE WRITING

Historical evidence suggests that picture writing of the sort just illustrated gradually became more formal and more abstract (see Diringer, 1962; Gelb, 1963). A circle, formerly used to represent the sun, could also be used to mean heat, light, day, or a god associated with the sun. Such stylised picture writing is known as "ideographic writing". For all its formality, it remains the case that a message in ideographic writing can be "read" in a wide variety of ways. True writing systems emerged for the first time when writing symbols were used to represent words of the language rather than objects or concepts. This important step has probably been taken independently in a number of places at different times. This is not to say that picture writing has become extinct in those cultures where writing has developed: road signs and manufacturers' symbolic instructions on household appliances are just two of the places where picture writing can still be seen today.

The earliest true writing systems (such as Sumerian cuneiform writing, developed in what is now southern Iraq between 4000 and 3000 BC) were based on the one-word-one-symbol principle. Such writing systems are called "logographic" (from the Greek *logos* meaning word) and individual symbols are known as "logograms". Modern Chinese remains logographic, as is one of the writing systems (*Kanji*) used in Japan (see Fig. 1.3). It is important that we should avoid equating logographic with less developed and alphabetic with more developed when thinking about writing. There are, for example, good reasons why Chinese should be written logographically. One is that the spoken Chinese language contains a great many *homophones*—words with different meanings which sound the same. If Chinese were written using an alphabet, these homophones would all be spelled the same, whereas a logographic writing system is able to use a visually distinct symbol for each distinct meaning. This is almost certainly of benefit to the reader of Chinese.

Many modern writing systems are, however, alphabetic; that is, they use a different letter, or a group of letters, to represent each distinctive sound in the spoken language. The first step in the development of the alphabet involved the logograms of early writing systems becoming progressively less and less picture-like. Their increasing arbitrariness may have fostered a change of attitude in readers and writers who may have

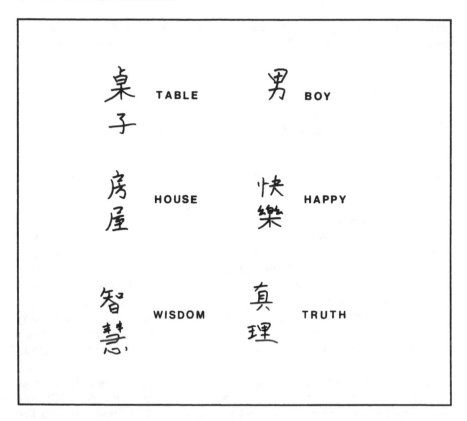

FIG. 1.3. Examples of Chinese logographs.

come to regard logograms less as representing concepts or meanings and more as representing words in the spoken language. When this transition happens, a logogram may be used not only for its original meaning, but also to represent a homophone with a different meaning but the same sound—as if a circle meaning SUN was also used to represent the word SON or, to borrow an example from Fromkin and Rodman (1974), as if two logograms for BEE and LEAF were combined to represent the abstract word BELIEF.

This use of logograms to represent word-sounds was taken a step further when the Egyptian logographic symbols were adopted by the Phoenecians, a people who lived on the eastern shores of the Mediterranean. They spoke an entirely different language from the Egyptians, but borrowed the Egyptian hieroglyphic symbols to represent the syllables of their own language. All connection between the symbols and their original meanings was now lost. In the hands of the Phoenecians, the conversion of an initially logographic writing system to a syllabic and sound-based one was completed (around 1500 BC).

The last major step towards the invention of the alphabet occurred around 1000 BC. That was when the ancient Greeks took over the syllabic Phoenecian writing system, adapting it by using a separate written character for each consonant and vowel sound of the Greek language. All modern alphabets are descendents of the Greek version (English comes from Greek via the Roman alphabet). To someone brought up with an alphabetic writing system, using letters to represent sounds may seem like a simple and obvious way to capture speech in visible form, but when thinking about reading and writing it is worth bearing in mind the fact that, as far as we know, the alphabetic principle has been invented just once in human history— by the Greeks around 1000 BC.

THE ORIGINS OF ENGLISH SPELLING

In what we might call a "transparent" alphabetic writing system, the spelling of each word conveys that word's pronunciation clearly and unambiguously. Some modern alphabets, such as Finnish and Italian, come close to being transparent in this way. English written words like DOG, SHIP and PISTOL are also transparent (or "regular") because their pronunciation is straightforwardly predictable from their spelling to anyone who knows the normal correspondences between English letters and sounds. However, as teachers are only too well aware, many written English words deviously conceal their pronunciations. One need only contemplate the mismatch between spelling and pronunciation in such "irregular" words as YACHT, DEBT, ISLAND, WOMEN, KNIGHT and COLONEL to appreciate the truth of this.

English has not always contained the sorts of irregularly spelled words we find in today's books. Before the Norman Conquest (AD 1066), a standard system of spellings was in use throughout the country. Regional variation in spelling later became the norm. By about AD 1400 English words were spelled as they were pronounced, varying from place to place as dialect pronunciations varied, but spellings were still all transparent when matched against local dialects.

The introduction in England of the first printing press (by William Caxton in 1476), and the subsequent rapid spread of the new technology, heralded a move back towards standardisation of spellings. Unfortunately, the transparency of English spelling was an early victim. For a start, many early printers were Dutch and did not always bother to ascertain how English speakers pronounced words. It was these printers who, for example, put the CH in YACHT (because the equivalent Dutch word contained a sound similar to that in the Scottish pronunciation of the word "loch"). Previously, the English spelling of YACHT had been YOTT.

To complicate matters further, there were at large in the fifteenth and sixteenth centuries influential spelling reformers. Present-day spelling reformers typically aspire to bring English spellings back into line with their pronunciations. Earlier spelling reformers had different aims: they wanted to alter spellings in such a way as to reflect the Latin or Greek origins of words (at the expense of transparency if necessary). In their hands, the spelling of DETTE was changed to DEBT, DOUTE to DOUBT, and SUTIL to SUBTLE in order to reflect the origins of those words in the Latin words *debitum*, *dubite* and *subtilis*, respectively. Sometimes the reformers got it wrong. They introduced a C into SCISSORS and SCYTHE because they thought (wrongly) that both words derived from the Latin word *scindere* (to cleave); similarly, we owe our modern spelling of ANCHOR to a false historical link with the Greek word *anchorite*. Other examples of false etymology are the S in ISLAND (formerly ILAND) and the H in HOUR (formerly OURE); neither of those letters has ever formed part of the English pronunciation of those words.

The process of standardising English spellings was more or less completed by the time the first dictionaries were produced in the eighteenth century, the best known of which is Dr Samuel Johnson's *Dictionary of the English Language* (1755). Dictionaries have many virtues, but they also have one major drawback. The pronunciations of words change down the years. They always have, and they always will. Spellings, in contrast, become sanctified by dictionaries and fossilised within them. In the absence of spelling reform, there is a tendency for spellings and pronunciations to gradually diverge, so that more and more spellings become "irregular", no longer reflecting pronunciation accurately. For example, in the seventeenth century, the words KNAVE and KNIFE were both pronounced with an initial "k", WOULD and SHOULD were pronounced with an "l", and a sound like the "ch" in "loch", and spelled GH, occurred in the pronunciation of RIGHT, LIGHT, BOUGHT, EIGHT and similar words. All of these words have changed their pronunciations over the last 300 years with the result that their spellings, once transparent and rational, have become irregular and apparently capricious.

This tendency for spellings and pronunciations gradually to diverge has been counterbalanced to a small degree by a converse tendency for the pronunciations of words to change to match their spellings, a process known as "spelling pronunciation". There is, for example, a whole cluster of English words whose spelling begins with H because of an ancient Latin influence, though none of their pronunciations began with a "h" when their spellings were devised. In some the H remains unpronounced (e.g. HEIR, HONOUR, HONEST, HOUR), but in others the presence of the initial H in the spelling has caused their pronunciation to be modified (e.g. HABIT, HOSPITAL, HUMOUR and HERITAGE, none of whose pronunciations contained an "h" in the seventeenth century). Other examples of pronunciation changing to accommodate to spelling are a switch from "t" to "th" in words like ANTHEM, AUTHOR and THEATRE, and the introduction of a "t" sound in the word OFTEN, which nowadays is only rarely given its original pronunciation of "offen".

ORTHOGRAPHY AND PHONOLOGY

Phonemes and Letters

Linguists refer to the writing system used by a language as its *orthography* and the sound structure of the language as its *phonology*. The different sounds that are used to distinguish words with distinct meanings are known as the *phonemes* of the language. A spoken language contains many different sounds, but only some of them are used to distinguish between words. The "k" sound in "keep" is slightly different from the "k" sound in "cool", the latter being produced further back in the mouth. In Arabic, those two different k's are used to distinguish between words with different meanings. We can say that the two k's are different phonemes in Arabic (because they can signal differences of meaning) and Arabic has different letters for them. In English, they are two variants of the same phoneme, and are therefore represented by the same letter.

English has over 40 phonemes but has inherited only 26 letters, so letters have to be combined to represent some of the phonemes (e.g. SH, CH, TH, OO, EE). Even words with regular spellings may not have the same numbers of letters as phonemes (e.g. THROAT has six letters but only four phonemes represented by TH, R, OA and T). But in many words of English, the correspondence between spelling and sound is still more indirect. For reasons outlined above, English orthography is nowadays far from transparent, containing many irregular spelling–sound correspondences, even in some of its most common words. At first blush this might seem clearly undesirable, but some have argued that all may not be for the bad (e.g. Albrow, 1972; Sampson, 1985). At least a proportion of the deviations from transparency may be justifiable, and even beneficial.

Advantages of Irregularity?

We have observed that modern Chinese benefits from being able to use a different logograph for each of its many homophones (words with different meanings but the same pronunciation). English has few logographs (&, £ and $ perhaps), but not many. It does, however, contain a surprising number of homophones (e.g. YOU–YEW, MEET–MEAT, PEAR–PAIR, IN–INN, WHICH–WITCH). If, as will be argued later, skilled readers can access the meanings of familiar words directly from their written forms, then there is a clear advantage to having distinct spellings for the different meanings of homophones. Inevitably this means that at least one member of a homophone pair is likely to have an irregular spelling. Thus, the second member of each of the homophone pairs TOO–TWO, SINE–SIGN, THREW–THROUGH and KERNEL–COLONEL has an irregular spelling.

In 1913, the Oxford philosopher Henry Bradley presented the case for English spelling, arguing that skilled readers "form direct associations between certain familiar groups of letters [i.e. word spellings] and the meanings which they represent", that "to an accomplished reader it does not ... matter a jot whether his native language is phonetically spelt or not" and that "the graphic differentiation of homophones ... render[s] written English a better instrument of expression". He felt compelled to admit, though, that the irregularities and inconsistencies of English spelling create problems for the learner ("There is no doubt that those unphonetic features of our spelling, which have their practical value for the educated adult, do add enormously to the difficulty of learning to read and write").

Chomsky and Halle (1968) noted another possible advantage of spelling–sound irregularity in certain contexts. The words SIGN and BOMB contain the silent letters G and B which render their spellings irregular. But SIGN and BOMB are related to the words SIGNATURE and BOMBARD in which those letters are pronounced. Retaining the silent letters in SIGN and BOMB increases the irregularity of English spelling but allows families of words that are related in meaning to show a family resemblance in their spellings.

The written words ROPE, ROBE and ROSE are all converted from singular to plural morpheme by the simple addition of the letter S. But listen closely to the pronunciation of "ropes", "robes" and "roses", and you will hear that "ropes" ends with the sound "s", "robes" with the sound "z" and "roses" with the syllable "iz". Truly regular spellings of the three plural forms might be ROPES, ROBEZ and ROSIZ, but such spellings would disguise the fact that all three are simple plurals. The same happens with past tenses of verbs: spelling reformers committed to regularity at all cost might re-spell FLAPPED, SOARED and GLIDED as FLAPT, SOARD and GLIDID, but in so doing they would lose the consistent signalling of the past tense ending by the letters -ED.

Baker (1980) reports an experiment in which volunteer individuals (who in psychology are conventionally known as "subjects") were asked to pretend that they were either linguists trying to capture the pronunciation of words as accurately as possible in their spellings, or spelling reformers trying to produce rational, intelligent spellings of words. When they were being linguists, the majority of subjects opted for the FLAPT/ROBEZ types of spellings, but when the same individuals were being spelling reformers, they opted to ignore differences in pronunciation and preserve a reliable correspondence between the plural, past tense and certain letters; that is, they opted to retain the existing spellings.

THE USES OF WRITING

If asked to list some of the uses of writing, we may tend to think of "high" cultural attainments such as novels, plays, poetry and (perhaps) great scientific works. If so, it is salutary to look back at what use was made of writing when it first evolved, and hence what motivated its original development. We have seen that the oldest known true writing developed in Sumeria (now southern Iraq) somewhere between 4000 and 3000 BC. Their writing was typically done on clay tablets using a wooden implement called a stylus. The examples of their writing that have survived record not poems and plays, but business transactions and administrative minutiae—who paid what to whom in return for which goods, who has and who has not paid their taxes, and so on. Sampson (1985, p. 48) comments that all the early scripts were "primarily or exclusively used for somewhat humdrum ... administrative purposes". To this day, writing remains vital to the smooth pursuit of commerce, trade and the law, and far more words are used in writing business memos than in writing novels.

But once an orthography is in place, it can be put to other than commercial uses. Myths, legends and stories, previously handed down orally from generation to generation, can now be committed to writing and preserved for ever. Written manuscripts can survive the disappearance of cultures and entire ways of life. We know far more about past societies that had writing than those that did not, because writing allows the members of those societies to speak to us across time and space in a way that no other mode of communication can. Things may be changing a little with the development of other technologies for recording sound and vision, but it remains the case that literacy opens the door to a vast range of social and cultural experiences that are barred to the illiterate person. It is vital that we understand the nature of the reading skill and find better ways to help the members of our society to acquire it and benefit from its use.

FURTHER READING

Gaur, A. (1987). *A history of writing*. London: The British Library.
Gelb, I.J. (1963). *A study of writing* (2nd ed.). Chicago: University of Chicago Press.

Sampson, G. (1985). *Writing systems*. London: Hutchinson.

Scragg, D.G. (1974). *A history of English spelling*. Manchester: Manchester University Press/New York: Barnes & Noble.

CHAPTER TWO

Skilled Word Recognition

Reading is a skill, and a difficult one at that. An extended apprenticeship is required in order to master it fully. We will consider the processes of skill acquisition—that is, how we learn to read—in Chapters 7 and 8, but there is a lot to be said for studying the end result first. That way you have a clear idea of where the apprentice is heading when he or she starts the learning process. This and the next chapter are concerned with aspects of *skilled* reading. This chapter summarises some of the research which analyses how a skilled reader converts written words into meanings and speech. Chapter 3 shows how psychologists have developed theories and models of visual word recognition that encompass and explain the research findings.

If you were to scan the many scientific journals that contain articles on reading, you could be forgiven for concluding that most reading involves pronouncing single words aloud, or perhaps deciding whether or not strings of letters displayed on a screen in front of you form real words. Psychologists who study reading find it convenient at times to focus their attention on what goes on when readers recognise individual words, and we shall have cause to look at the results of such research at many points in this book, but we should never lose track of the fact that reading in its natural state involves reading sentences that link up to form passages of coherent, connected text which inform, instruct or perhaps just entertain.

EYE MOVEMENTS IN READING

The starting point of text reading is the movement of the eyes over the page. We shall accordingly begin our survey of skilled reading with a consideration of the characteristics of the eye movements made by skilled readers.

Sit facing someone you know and ask them to keep their eyes on the tip of your finger as you move it in front of them from left to right and back again. If you watch their eyes you will see that they move smoothly to and fro. Now ask your assistant to repeat the same eye movements, but this time in the absence of any moving object to follow. To the person making the eye movements they will probably feel just the same as before, but you will be able to see that the movements are no longer smooth, but instead progress from side to side in a series of quick jerks with brief moments of stillness in between.

The fact is that however hard you try, you can only move your eyes smoothly if you are tracking an object that is itself moving. Otherwise the jerk-and-pause movement pattern occurs. Printed text stays still while the eyes roam over it, and because the text is still, the eye movement pattern of readers involves jerks and pauses. In the world of reading research, the jerks that move the eyes forwards or backwards are known as "saccades" and the pauses as "fixations". Figure 2.1 shows in somewhat idealised form the eye movements that a skilled reader might make when reading a passage of text. Fixations are represented by circles above the fixated word, with larger circles denoting longer fixations. Saccades are represented by arrows.

There are a number of things to be noticed in Fig. 2.1. The first is that most words in the passage are fixated. Short, predictable words like *a, the* or *and* may be skipped over, but the majority of words attract at least a brief fixation. That said, fixations vary considerably in their duration—the typical range being about 150–500 msec with an average of 200–250 msec (i.e. about a quarter of a second). We will consider shortly some of the factors that cause one fixation to be shorter or longer than another.

Saccades are much quicker, lasting only 20–50 msec. As long ago as 1900, Dodge established that you see little or nothing during a saccade. Even a strong flash of light may not be perceived if it coincides with a saccade (Latour, 1962). It is during fixations that the reader extracts visual information from the printed page.

Not all saccades take the reader forward through a text. Although not depicted in Fig. 2.1, in fact some 10–15% of saccades involve regressive, backward movements of the eyes. There are a number of reasons why a regressive eye movement may occur. A reader, especially a relatively unskilled one, may have skipped too far forward and may need to go back

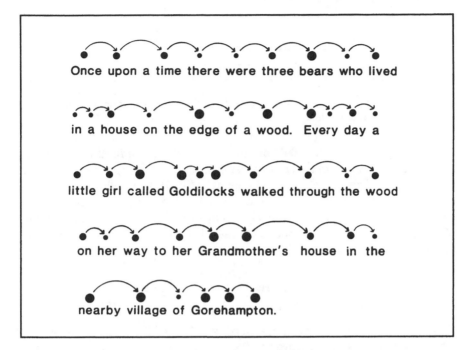

FIG. 2.1. The pattern of eye movements that a skilled reader might make in reading a passage of text. Circles represent fixations, with larger circles indicating longer fixations, and arrows represent saccades. (For simplification we have omitted the 10% or so of backward, "regressive" eye movements that occur in natural reading.)

a few spaces in order to fixate a word properly. Alternatively, a reader may have failed to understand a phrase or sentence and will need to make a regressive eye movement to have another go at the difficult section.

Close inspection of Fig. 2.1 will also reveal that the fixation dots are not positioned centrally over their words. The skilled reader causes the eyes to come to rest somewhere between the beginning and middle of a word (Rayner, 1979). A clue as to why the "convenient viewing position" (O'Regan, 1981) might be only two or three letters into a word comes from research investigating the area of uptake of visual information around the point of fixation. Rayner, Well, and Pollatsek (1980) showed that visual information is not absorbed symmetrically around the fixation point; rather, readers of English take in more information to the right than to the left of fixation. The "perceptual span"—the name given to the region of information uptake during a fixation—extends some 15 or so letters or spaces to the right of the fixation point, but only 3 or 4 to the left (see Fig. 2.2 for an illustration of this).

Actually, it makes sense for the reader of English to have a lop-sided window on the printed world. Letters and words to the left of fixation have

FIG. 2.2. The "perceptual span" in reading typically extends further to the right of the fixation point than to the left.

already been identified and do not need to be processed further. It is more efficient to concentrate visual processing on those upcoming words that fall to the right of fixation. Readers of languages like Hebrew whose script runs right to left show the opposite asymmetry. They pick up more information to the left of fixation than to the right, showing that the asymmetry of the perceptual span is a consequence of learning to read (Pollatsek, Bolozky, Well, & Rayner, 1981).

FACTORS AFFECTING THE EASE OR DIFFICULTY OF WORD RECOGNITION

We have already noted that some words are fixated for longer than others. This suggests that some words are recognised more easily than others. A great deal of psychological research has gone into identifying the factors that determine ease or difficulty of word recognition. This research feeds directly into the development of theories and models of word recognition in reading (see Chapter 3), so we shall spend a little time here on factors affecting word recognition.

Familiarity

However well read a person may be, there will be words in the language that he or she has never come across. The psychologist who wants to compare the recognition of familiar words with the recognition of unfamiliar words faces a problem, however, because a word that is unfamiliar to one person may be familiar to another. One way out of this dilemma is to invent your own "unfamiliar words". It is not difficult to combine letters together to form strings that could be words but happen not to be (e.g. WIB, FLONT or OMBRILLA). Such invented words are referred to in the psychological literature as "pseudowords" or "nonwords", and turn out to be surprisingly useful, not only in the exploration of skilled reading, but also of disordered reading and the process of learning to read.

Learning a new word causes it to change from being strange and meaningless into something which looks familiar, conveys a meaning and has a known pronunciation. To the cognitive psychologist, learning a new word involves creating "internal representations" of that word's appearance, meaning and sound, and linking those representations one to another.

A variety of different experimental techniques has been used to show that once a word has become familiar, it is actually *perceived* more easily than an unknown word or nonword. For example, if subjects are shown two words or two nonwords one above the other and simply have to press one button if the two are the same and another button if they are different (e.g. VIB and VIB are two nonwords that are the same; CAR and CAP are two words that are different), then responses are faster for pairs of words than for pairs of nonwords (Eichelman, 1970).

If the task is simply to read words or nonwords aloud as rapidly as possible, familiar words are read faster than nonwords (Glushko, 1979). Given that finding, one can ask if the reason SEAT is read aloud faster than SEAB is because the written nonword SEAB is an unfamiliar combination of letters or because the spoken nonword "seab" is an unfamiliar combination of phonemes that is harder to pronounce. This question can be answered by comparing the speed of reading SEAT with the speed of reading SEET, where both have the same pronunciation, but only one is familiar in its written form. It turns out that familiar words are read aloud faster even than "pseudohomophones" (!) like SEET (McCann & Besner, 1987). Hence, the slower reading of nonwords than words is due (at least in part) to the lack of internal representations of the visual form of nonwords.

Frequency

Even among familiar words, some are more familiar than others. Tables exist showing the number of times different words occur in samples of written English (e.g. Hofland & Johansson, 1988; Kucera & Francis, 1967). These tables can be used to select words that differ on frequency of occurrence in the language, allowing comparisons to be made between the recognition of common, "high-frequency" words and less common, "low-frequency" words. We should note that "low-frequency" words are still familiar words; for example, BRAWL, MANICURE, TAPE and YACHT all occur less than 10 times per million words in typical written English, and hence would be classed as low-frequency words in most experiments.

The psychological literature abounds with reports that high-frequency words are easier to recognise than low-frequency words (see Monsell, 1991). An early demonstration of this was given by Preston (1935). She showed words one at a time to skilled readers (students at the University of Minnesota) who were instructed to read each one aloud as rapidly as possible. Preston measured the time between the initial presentation of a word and the onset of each subject's pronunciation of that word, and was able to show that the average "naming latency" for high-frequency words was less than that for low-frequency words.

Faced with such a report, one can begin to ask questions about the origins of the frequency effect within the mental processes responsible for reading(see Monsell, 1991). For example, are high-frequency words actually recognised faster than low-frequency words, or is that they are simply easier to speak aloud? This particular question can be addressed by looking to see whether frequency effects can be found in tasks that do not require overt pronunciation of the words used in the experiment. One such task is the "lexical decision task". In a typical lexical decision experiment, subjects are shown strings of letters one at a time. Some letter strings are familiar words; others are invented nonwords. They come in an unpredictable order. The subject sits with his or her hands poised over two buttons and is instructed to press one button as quickly as possible if the letter string is a word and another if it is a nonword. The time between the initial appearance of a word or nonword and the subject pressing the appropriate button is the "reaction time". Reaction times will be averaged over many words and subjects to establish that any differences observed are not idiosyncratic properties of particular words or particular readers.

The subject in a lexical decision task does not speak the words aloud, yet effects of word frequency continue to be observed in the form of faster reaction times to high- than low-frequency words (e.g. Forster & Chambers, 1973; Monsell, Doyle, & Haggard, 1989). The size of the difference is at least as great as that seen for naming speed, suggesting that the effect may genuinely reflect ease or difficulty of recognition, not just naming. Reports of shorter fixation durations on high- than low-frequency words in the reading of passages of text are compatible with this suggestion (Inhoff & Rayner, 1986; Rayner & Duffy, 1986).

Age of Acquisition

Other experiments suggest that, all other things being equal, words learned early in life may be recognised more easily than words learned later. For example, Gilhooly and Logie (1981) and Coltheart, Laxon, and Keating (1988) showed that early-learned words are read aloud more rapidly than late-acquired words. The same is true of the time required to name pictures of objects, where objects whose names are learned early in life are named faster than objects with late-acquired names (Carroll & White, 1973; Morrison, Ellis, & Quinlan, 1992). This has led to the suggestion that the two effects have a common source which lies within those psychological processes involved in accessing the pronunciations of both objects and written words. The spoken forms of words learned early in life may be retrieved more quickly and more efficiently than words learned later (Brown & Watson, 1987; Gilhooly & Watson, 1981).

It is easy to assert that all other things being equal, early-acquired words are processed more rapidly than late-acquired words, but proving it is rendered more difficult than one might first imagine by the fact that words learned early in life also tend to be words that are used more frequently thereafter. A set of words selected for being high frequency will also tend to be words learned earlier in life than the words in a set chosen for being low frequency. For that matter, they will also tend to be shorter words with more concrete meanings because longer, more abstract words tend to be words of lower frequency. A great deal of care and attention must be devoted to the design and analysis of experiments if one is to establish beyond reasonable doubt that an observed effect is genuinely attributable to age of acquisition, word frequency, word length or concreteness of meaning, and not to one of the other members of that list. Indeed, at the time of writing, there is debate over the possibility that effects attributed in the past to word frequency might actually be effects of age of acquisition. For example, some words may be named faster than others because they are learned earlier, rather than because they are of higher frequency.

Repetition

Factors like frequency, age of acquisition, length and concreteness are stable properties of a word that will affect ease of recognition whenever a word is encountered. But we also know that ease of recognition can change from occasion to occasion in response to more local factors. One such factor is simple repetition. A familiar word encountered for the second or third time in a task is recognised more easily than a word encountered for the first time. This is true whether the task is reading aloud or lexical decision (Monsell, 1985). It is not necessary for a word to be seen in the same format on each occasion; reading the word DESK will facilitate later recognition of desk, *desk*, DESK or *DESK* (Carr, Brown, & Charalambous, 1989; Clarke & Morton, 1983). However, hearing the spoken word "desk" or seeing a picture of a desk has little or no effect on subsequent recognition of the written word DESK (Jackson & Morton, 1984; Warren & Morton, 1982). Something happens within the reading system when a reader reads DESK that affects subsequent recognition of desk, *desk*, DESK or *DESK*, but that something is confined to the reading system and does not affect the mental processes responsible for recognising spoken words or objects. Consideration of what that "something" might be will be deferred until Chapter 3.

Meaning and Context

Back in 1897, Pillsbury reported that subjects will recognise a written word more easily if they have just heard a different word that is related in meaning to the one now being read. Sadly, Pillsbury's observation, like many others of its day, was soon forgotten, and modern interest in "semantic priming" stems more from the work of Meyer and Schvaneveldt (1971). They showed subjects pairs of letter strings which were either both real words, both invented nonwords or one word and one nonword. In a variation on the usual lexical decision procedure, the subjects were required to press one button if *both* strings were words, and another button otherwise. Meyer and Schvaneveldt found that when both strings were words, the subjects responded faster and more accurately when the two were also related in meaning (e.g. BREAD and BUTTER compared with DOCTOR and BUTTER). Subsequent studies have shown that semantic priming occurs in a wide range of different tasks and situations. Subjects are, for example, faster at naming words that are preceded by a related word, and faster to make lexical decisions to primed words (Neely, 1991).

Now, the single word BREAD is a somewhat minimalist "context" for the word BUTTER. Other studies of context effects have examined the effects of presenting a word in a sentence or longer piece of text where the word is either in harmony with the meaning of its context or somewhat dissonant. Tulving and Gold (1963) measured the "visual duration threshold" of words presented either in isolation or after one, two, four or eight words of preceding context. The context words were either appropriate or inappropriate to the test word. So, in the eight-word, appropriate context condition of this experiment, subjects read a context such as *The skiers were buried alive by the sudden ...* and were then shown a target word such as *avalanche* very briefly. If the target word was not identified correctly, the context was repeated and the target word was presented again at a longer exposure. This procedure continued until the target word was correctly recognised and its "threshold" was noted. Tulving and Gold found that relevant contexts lowered visual duration thresholds, i.e. made target words easier to identify. Increasing the amount of relevant context from one to eight words increased the size of the facilitation observed. Irrelevant context (e.g. *Medieval knights in battle were noted for their ... avalanche)* actually made target words harder to identify than when they were presented in isolation. That is, relevant context facilitated word identification, whereas irrelevant context inhibited recognition.

Tulving and Gold's experiment has been criticised on the grounds that repeatedly presenting the context may encourage subjects to guess at the target word using the context plus such letters from the target word as they think they may have perceived. Thus, reading *The skiers were buried alive by the sudden ...*, then seeing fleetingly a longish word beginning av- and ending -he, may be enough to encourage many subjects to respond "avalanche". More recent experiments have sought to overcome this objection by presenting the context sentences and terminating words only once, requiring subjects to make a rapid naming or lexical decision response to the final word. Under these circumstances, faster recognition responses continue to be reported when the word being responded to fits the preceding context than when the preceding context is either neutral or positively misleading (e.g. Schuberth & Eimas, 1977; Stanovich & West, 1979).

But even these experiments are some steps removed from normal reading. The context experiments which come closest to the situation of normal reading are those which have measured eye movements to words that vary in the extent to which they are compatible with their context. Ehrlich and Rayner (1981) found that fixation durations on key words in passages of text were shortened by about 30–50 msec when the words meshed with their context than when they did not. Indeed, readers often skipped completely over words that were highly predictable. Thus, useful context would seem to aid word identification even in a situation that approximates normal reading as closely as possible.

Spelling–Sound Regularity

We noted in Chapter 1 that there was a time in the history of the English language when the spellings of all words were an accurate reflection of their pronunciations. We also noted that a variety of factors have conspired to ensure that that is no longer the case. The result is that we now have some "regular" words which retain a good match between spelling and pronunciation, but also many "irregular" words whose spelling and pronunciation are ill-matched.

In fact, the situation is a little more complex than that. There are varieties and degrees of irregularity that need to be taken into account. Some irregular words *look* bizarre—words like YACHT, TSAR or GAUGE. Other irregular words look perfectly normal. For example, HAVE, PINT and THREAT all look like standard English words, but HAVE is deemed to be irregular because -AVE is usually pronounced as in SAVE, GAVE and BRAVE; PINT is irregular because -INT is usually pronounced as in HINT, MINT and TINT; and THREAT is irregular because -EAT is usually pronounced as in BEAT, HEAT and TREAT.

Words with consistent spelling–sound relations are read aloud more rapidly by skilled readers than words whose spelling–sound relations are inconsistent. The advantage that regular, consistent words enjoy in naming speed does not, however, extend to lexical decision speed once words with unusual appearances are excluded (Coltheart, Besner, Jonasson, & Davelaar, 1979; Seidenberg, Waters, Barnes, & Tanenhaus, 1984). That is, although an unconventional appearance may make a word harder to perceive (Parkin, 1982), there is no evidence that consistency of spelling–sound correspondence *per se* affects the perceptibility of words, only the speed with which they can be read aloud.

Interactions

We have discussed factors like repetition, context, frequency and regularity independently of one another, but they also combine together in ways that need to be explained. For example, the effects of repetition and regularity on recognition are both greater for uncommon (low-frequency) than common (high-frequency) words. Repeating a low-frequency word improves the speed of recognition much more than does repeating a high-frequency word (Scarborough, Cortese, & Scarborough, 1977). Similarly, the fact of having an irregular spelling retards the naming of low-frequency words but has relatively little effect on the naming speeds of high-frequency words (Seidenberg et al., 1984; Taraban & McClelland, 1987). Theoretical accounts of how repetition, frequency, regularity, etc., exert their collective influences on word recognition must account not only for the basic effects of these factors, but also for the way they interact with one another.

Another case in point relates to the effects of priming from sentence contexts or from semantically related words. Stanovich and West (1979; 1983) showed that appropriate sentence contexts prime word recognition more when print is hard to read than when it is clear. Semantic priming effects between pairs of words are also greater for "degraded" than clearly printed words, whether the task used to demonstrate priming is lexical decision or speeded naming (Becker & Killion, 1977). Both sentence and single-word semantic priming are also greater for low-frequency words than high-frequency words (Becker, 1979; Schuberth & Eimas, 1977). Finally, younger or less skilled readers show larger sentence priming effects than more skilled readers (West & Stanovich, 1978). Stanovich (1980; 1981) drew these various findings together in his "interactive compensatory" theory. He proposed that word recognition by skilled readers dealing with common words that are clearly written is so fast and automatic that contextual priming is unnecessary. Where context becomes helpful is when word recognition is slowed down and rendered more effortful. This can be as a result of poor print quality, or because the words are of low frequency, or because the reader is unskilled. In any of these circumstances, word recognition slows to the point where context becomes helpful and facilitatory.

That completes our brief look at the factors that affect ease or difficulty of word recognition. As stated earlier, the results of experiments like those just reviewed have played an important part in shaping theories and models of word recognition. It is to those theories and models that we turn next.

FURTHER READING

Besner, D. & Humphreys, G.W. (Eds.). (1991). *Basic processes in reading: Visual word recognition.* Hillsdale, NJ: Lawrence Erlbaum Associates Inc.

Henderson, L. (1982). *Orthography and word recognition in reading.* London: Academic Press.

Humphreys, G.W. & Bruce, V. (1989). *Visual cognition: Computational, experimental and neuropsychological perspectives.* Hove: Lawrence Erlbaum Associates Ltd.

Patterson, K. & Coltheart, V. (1987). Phonological processes in reading: A tutorial review. In M. Coltheart (Ed.), *Attention and performance XII: The psychology of reading.* Hove: Lawrence Erlbaum Associates Ltd.

Rayner, K. & Pollatsek, A. (1989). *The psychology of reading.* Englewood Cliffs, NJ: Prentice-Hall.

CHAPTER THREE

Models of Word Recognition

Models of word recognition are attempts to characterise some of the mental processes that allow a reader to identify, comprehend and pronounce written words. They try to decompose the act of word recognition into its component parts and describe the workings of those parts. An example of such a model is the influential "logogen model" developed by John Morton in a series of papers (e.g. Morton, 1964a; 1969; 1979). Though detailed and formalised, the logogen model existed only on paper and in the minds of its users. More recent models of word recognition have been expressed in the form of computer programs which aim to mimic (or "simulate") aspects of human word recognition. Examples of this latter genre are the models of McClelland and Rumelhart (1981), Sejnowski and Rosenberg (1988), Seidenberg and McClelland (1989) and Hinton and Shallice (1981).

Look at a page of a book or newspaper written in an unfamiliar script and an unfamiliar language (which might, for you, be Arabic or Chinese) and all you will see are meaningless black squiggles on a white background. Look at a page of a book or newspaper written in your own language and script and the words leap out at you, carrying with them their meanings and sounds. When we finally understand all there is to understand about reading, the theoretical model we settle on will explain why the latter experience is so radically different from the former. It will explain how different squiggles are recognised as letters, and how certain combinations of letters are recognised as familiar words while others convey nothing. It will explain the differences in recognition speed and accuracy that we noted in the previous chapter between familiar words and nonwords, and why letters embedded in familiar words are identified more easily. It will explain why we may be better able to recognise words that are of high frequency of occurrence, early age of acquisition, or are presented repeatedly or in appropriate semantic contexts. It will explain why words with consistent spelling–sound correspondences are named more rapidly that less regular words, but are not classified as words any faster in a lexical decision task. And so on. We are still some way from settling upon the ultimate model of word recognition, but a start has been made.

A SIMPLE MODEL FOR WORD RECOGNITION IN READING

The model which will be presented in this chapter and referred back to many times in the remainder of the book makes no claims to originality, being distilled from several of the models in current circulation. It tries to extract and emphasise the areas of broad agreement and to skate lightly over the areas of contention. The model is shown in diagrammatic form in Fig. 3.1. As already mentioned, the idea behind such models is that word recognition is the product of orchestrated activity that occurs within a number of cognitive sub-systems which operate at least partially independently one from another. Such semi-independent cognitive sub-systems are sometimes referred to as "modules" (Fodor, 1983). The concept of modularity is an important one. For example, if the different operations involved in word recognition are handled by different cognitive modules, then brain injury or abnormal development may result in readers in whom some aspects of reading are reasonably normal while others are impaired. The pattern of intact and impaired aspects of reading may differ between individuals, producing different patterns of reading disorder. We may, indeed, be able to learn something about the normal reading model from a study of reading disorders. We shall explore this possibility as it applies to acquired dyslexia in Chapter 4 and to developmental dyslexia in Chapter 8.

The Visual Analysis System and the Visual Input Lexicon

The first cognitive module of Fig. 3.1 that is involved in processing a printed word is the *visual analysis system*. That system has two main duties. The first is to identify squiggles on a printed page as different letters of the alphabet. The output of the visual analysis system may consist of "abstract letter identities" (Coltheart, 1981), which should not to be confused with

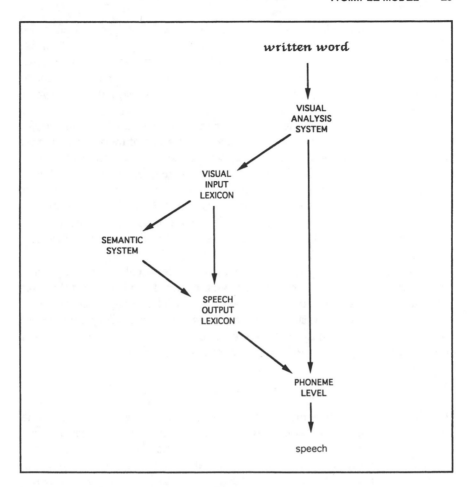

FIG. 3.1. Simple functional model of some of the cognitive processes involved in recognising single written words.

either letter names or letter sounds. Abstract letter identities are representations which distinguish one letter from another while ignoring the different shapes that a letter can take. Thus, the output of the visual analysis system will be the same for desk, *desk*, DESK and *DESK*.

The second and related duty of the visual analysis system is to note the *position* of each letter in its word. Many pairs of words in English are distinguished only by the order in which their letters occur. Examples range from POT and TOP to ORCHESTRA and CARTHORSE. Only by tagging each abstract letter identity with its position in the word in which it is embedded can the reading system distinguish between such word pairs.

The visual analysis system must encode letter identities and positions before the reader can determine whether a word being fixated is familiar or unfamiliar and, if familiar, which word it is. The operations of the visual analysis system are required whether the string of letters on the page forms a highly familiar word, a real but visually unfamiliar word, or a psychologist's invented nonword.

The task of identifying letter strings as familiar words is the responsibility of the *visual input lexicon*[1]. It is a sort of mental word-store which contains representations of the written forms of all familiar words. The representations within the visual input lexicon may be termed "word recognition units". There will be a visual word recognition unit for the familiar word TOP but not for the nonword TEP, for MADE but not MAPE, and for FOX but not PHOKS or FEX. The visual input lexicon serves as a gateway to word meanings and pronunciations, but does not itself contain meanings or pronunciations.

Becoming familiar with new written words involves creating new recognition units for them in the visual input lexicon and forming associative connections between those units and the representations of meanings and pronunciations. This is an important part of learning to read. As we shall see in Chapter 8, some children have great difficulty with precisely this aspect of the acquisition of literacy skills.

Beyond the Visual Input Lexicon

In Fig. 3.1, the arrow connecting the visual analysis system to the visual input lexicon is bi-directional. This is meant to indicate that not only can information (or activation) flow inwards from the visual analysis system to the visual input lexicon, but it can also flow back in the opposite direction. That is, activity within recognition units can feed back down to letter identification and influence that process. Familiar words have recognition units in the visual input lexicon whereas nonwords do not, so the visual analysis system will enjoy the benefit of "top-down" support from the lexicon when a familiar word is being analysed but not when the letter string being processed is a nonword. We saw in the previous chapter that letters in words seem to be perceived more easily than the same letters embedded in nonwords. The concept of a "top-down" contribution from higher processes and stores (such as the visual input lexicon) to lower ones (such as the visual analysis system) explains how such effects might arise. McClelland and Rumelhart's (1981) computer simulation of word recognition shows how the perceptual superiorities enjoyed by words over nonwords that were discussed in the previous chapter (e.g. faster same–different responses to pairs of words than to pairs of nonwords) can be modelled very neatly with the aid of these top-down influences.

The visual input lexicon of Fig. 3.1 is shown as having two outputs. The output to the component labelled *speech output lexicon*[2] has to do with accessing the pronunciations of words and will be discussed shortly. The output to the component labelled *semantic system* is the one of immediate concern and has to do with accessing the meaning of a word being read. The semantic system is the repository of all knowledge about the meanings of familiar words. Discussion of just what internal representations of the meanings of words might consist of can be found in Garnham (1985) and Johnson-Laird (1987).

On reading the word FOX, the visual analysis system tells you that the letters are F1, O2 and X3. The visual input lexicon tells you that this string of letters is one you have encountered before. But it is the semantic system that contains the knowledge that a FOX is a four-legged mammal of medium size with reddish fur and a bushy tail which lives in holes, has a reputation for cunning and is bad news for chickens. The goal of normal reading is to comprehend what is being read, and that requires the activation of word meanings in the semantic system. It is commonly assumed that the same semantic system is involved in understanding both written and spoken words (avoiding what would otherwise be an enormous duplication of semantic information). The operation of the semantic system can be tapped experimentally by a range of tasks such as asking readers to decide whether or not a word belongs in a pre-specified category (e.g. FRUIT–PEAR *vs* FRUIT–BEAR) or whether two words have similar or dissimilar meanings (GIFT–DONATION *vs* GIFT–VOCATION).

The connection between the visual input lexicon and the semantic system is again bi-directional, allowing top-down influences of word meanings on word identification. This helps to explain sentence context effects in word identification and semantic priming. Suppose you have just read the word NURSE. Your visual analysis system has correctly encoded the letters as N1, U2, R3, S4, E5 and that input has correctly activated the recognition unit for NURSE in the visual input lexicon. Connections from the visual input lexicon to the semantic system cause the meaning of NURSE to be activated within the semantic system. A common assumption is that activation spreads laterally from one concept to other related concepts within the semantic system (Collins & Loftus, 1975). Hence, activating the meaning of NURSE will cause the meanings of related words such as HOSPITAL, DOCTOR and PATIENT to become active. Activation will pass back down the link from the semantic system to the visual input lexicon and will "warm up" the recognition units for HOSPITAL, DOCTOR and PATIENT. The result is that if the next word to come along happens to be DOCTOR, less input from the visual analysis system will be required in order to identify it, and recognition will occur more rapidly. This is the phenomenon of semantic priming and priming of words in appropriate sentence contexts that we discussed in the previous chapter.

We also noted in the previous chapter that words encountered frequently in reading may be recognised faster than less frequently encountered words, and that repeated presentations of words also facilitate recognition. Several accounts of word recognition propose that those two phenomena are closely related and require a single explanation. Morton suggested that individual "logogens" (his name for word recognition units in the visual input lexicon) have variable thresholds. A logogen's threshold determines the amount of activity that must be present within it before it will "fire" and cause a word to be recognised. Morton further suggested that each time a logogen fires, its threshold is lowered, only returning gradually to its previous level. If a word is encountered for a second time before the threshold on its logogen has returned to resting level, less visual information will be needed to cause that logogen to fire and the word to be recognised. That is the phenomenon of repetition priming. The threshold on the logogen for a word which, because of its high frequency of occurrence in the language, is constantly being encountered, will hover permanently below resting level. The more frequent the word, the lower its threshold will be. That is the word frequency effect.

One encounter with a low-frequency word may substantially lower its threshold, but the threshold on the logogen for a high-frequency word may be so low already that one additional encounter with the word will have little or no measurable consequence. That is the interaction between repetition and word frequency that was mentioned in Chapter 2. The already low threshold of logogens for high-frequency words (and the correspondingly high state of readiness) will also serve to diminish the effect of contextual and semantic priming. We noted in Chapter 2 that frequency interacts with context and semantic priming in precisely this way.

The semantic system contains everything you know about a FOX except how to pronounce the word "fox". That knowledge is contained within a separate word store, the speech output lexicon. If you were to see a picture of a fox rather than the written word FOX, then you would name the animal by first activating your store of semantic knowledge in the semantic system, then by using the connections between the semantic system and the speech output lexicon to retrieve the appropriate name. Because a fox is a reasonably familiar creature, you are unlikely to struggle to remember the name, but everyone experiences from time to time the frustration of not being able to recall the name of something whose "meaning" (size, shape, function, properties, etc.) are known. You know that you know the name, which may hover tantalisingly on the tip of your tongue, but you are temporarily unable to bring it to mind. In terms of our model, that experience arises when semantic information fails to activate the entry for the required word in the speech output lexicon. The experience itself serves to illustrate the separateness and dissociability of word meanings from spoken word-forms.

We noted in Chapter 2 that words learned early in life are produced more rapidly in both object naming and reading aloud. The speech output lexicon is involved in both of these tasks, and it has been suggested that age of acquisition effects arise because the representations of early-acquired words in the speech output lexicon can be accessed more quickly than can the representations of late-acquired words (see Brown & Watson, 1987; Gilhooly & Watson, 1981).

From Print to Sound via Meaning

One way to read a word aloud is to employ the route from print to sound that passes though the visual input lexicon, the semantic system and the speech output lexicon. We might refer to this as "reading via meaning". There is considerable evidence to suggest that when people are reading text aloud (as distinct from single words), then reading does indeed occur via meaning. For example, Morton (1964b) asked skilled readers to read aloud passages of text that varied in their degree of approximation to normal English. A total of 133 errors were noted in which a word in the text was replaced in the act of reading aloud by another word of similar meaning (for example, misreading Sunday as "Saturday", might as "may", evening as "morning" and came as "gone"). Levin and Kaplan (1970) made similar observations. These semantic errors in text reading imply that the meaning of the text is being extracted *before* it is converted into speech; that is, that reading aloud is being "semantically mediated". In terms of our model, this means that written words in text first activate their meanings in the semantic system, and that those meanings are then used to retrieve the appropriate spoken word-forms from the speech output lexicon.

There are certain words within the English language that can *only* be read aloud correctly via activation of meaning. Read the following short passage: *She was deeply unhappy. The material of her dress had a large tear in it, and in the corner of her eye a tear was forming.* The letter string T1, E2, A3, R4 occurs twice but is pronounced differently according to whether it refers to a rip in some material or a droplet of water that rolls down the cheek. The point is that a reader must know which meaning is implied in a given portion of text before he or she can know which pronunciation is appropriate. TEAR (in the eye) and TEAR (in a dress) are known technically as "homographic heterophones" (!). They are homographic because they are spelt the same but heterophones because they are pronounced differently. Other examples are SOW (the female pig) and SOW (some seeds), BASS (a deep-voiced singer) and BASS (a fish), and MINUTE (an interval of time) and MINUTE (very small). Such words can only be read aloud correctly by first activating the relevant meaning in the semantic system, then using the meaning as the basis for selecting the correct pronunciation from the speech output lexicon.

These are experimental and technical arguments for the fact of reading text via meaning, but we should also note that reading aloud involves modifying one's tone of voice to suit the changing mood of the text, letting the voice rise and fall according to whether the sentence being read is a statement or a question, pausing for effect or to mark a change of topic, and so on. All these features that distinguish skilled reading aloud from mere barking at print are features that depend on understanding the text before you speak it; in other words, features that depend on reading via meaning.

Direct Associations Between Print and Sound for Whole Words

We have noted the existence in Fig. 3.1 of a direct connection between the visual input lexicon and the speech output lexicon. The visual input lexicon contains representations that are activated by familiar words, while the speech output lexicon contains the pronunciations of familiar words. Connections between corresponding entries in the visual input lexicon and the speech output lexicon create direct associations between print and sound for familiar words, associations that bypass the representations of word meanings contained within the semantic system. All current models of word recognition incorporate such associations, and in many this is the only portion to have been implemented as a working computer simulation (e.g. McClelland & Rumelhart, 1981; Seidenberg & McClelland, 1989; Sejnowski & Rosenberg, 1988).

Unlike the situation in text reading, there is little evidence to suggest that word meanings are actively involved in reading aloud when the task is one of reading single words as quickly as possible. For example, whenever word meanings are involved in the performance of a task, words with concrete, tangible meanings tend to be processed faster than words with more abstract meanings, yet there is little or no effect of abstractness of meaning on the time required to read single words aloud (Coltheart et al., 1988; Gilhooly & Logie, 1981). We will also review in Chapter 4 reports of brain-damaged patients who remain able to read words aloud while showing little or no comprehension of the meanings of the words they read. Such patients have been taken as further evidence of the existence of direct connections between visual word recognition (the visual input lexicon) and pronunciations (the speech output lexicon).

If such direct associations between print and sound exist, we might ask what contribution they play in the reading of text. One possibility is that the input to the speech output lexicon that comes from the visual input lexicon combines with input from the semantic system to determine word choice. It may, for example, serve the purpose of helping select between words with very similar meanings (e.g. RUG and MAT or BUCKET and PAIL) and so help reduce the number of semantic reading errors that might otherwise occur.

The Phoneme Level

A long word like "hippopotamus" or "neuropsychology" is presumed to be retrieved in one go from the speech output lexicon as a sequence of distinctive speech sounds (phonemes). But the phonemes of "hippo-potamus" cannot be articulated all at once—they must be converted from first to last into a co-ordinated sequence of articulatory movements. Hence we need to postulate some form of short-term store in which phonemes can be held in the interval between being retrieved from the speech output lexicon and being articulated. That short-term store is what in Fig. 3.1 is called the *phoneme level*.[3] Studies of natural, spontaneous speech (as distinct from reading aloud) suggest that several words corresponding to a phrase or short sentence may be retrieved from the speech output lexicon and may be held simultaneously at the phoneme level awaiting articulation (Ellis & Beattie, 1986). Hence we must endow the phoneme level with a capacity sufficient to hold strings of several words if need be.

Is the storage of more than one word in phonemic form required in reading? One line of argument suggests that it is. If you keep a record of the location of eye fixations as a skilled reader reads aloud a passage of text and, at the same, note at each point what the voice is saying, then you will notice that the eyes stay ahead of the voice for much of the time. There is typically a gap of a few words between what is being fixated and what is being spoken. This is called the "eye–voice span" (Levin, 1979). Morton (1964b) suggested that the words within the eye–voice span—words the eyes have fixated but the voice has not yet spoken—are the contents of the phoneme level (or, as he called it, the *response buffer*) at any given time.

LEXICAL VERSUS SUBLEXICAL ROUTES
FROM PRINT TO SOUND

We have outlined two procedures capable of converting familiar words from print to sound. One is reading via meaning, where semantic representations mediate between print and sound. In terms of Fig. 3.1, this route is *written word* → visual analysis system → visual input lexicon

→ semantic system → speech output lexicon → phoneme level → speech. The second procedure is non-semantic reading in which the semantic system is bypassed by direct connections between the visual input lexicon and the speech output lexicon. Thus, the route is *written word* → visual analysis system → visual input lexicon → speech output lexicon → phoneme level → speech.

Both of these procedures require that the words being read are represented in the visual input lexicon. That is, they can only operate on words that are already familiar. But skilled readers are not completely stymied by words that are unfamiliar in their printed forms. Any skilled reader can make a stab at reading aloud an unfamiliar string of letters and may be able to recognise the word on the basis of its sound. That process cannot involve the visual input lexicon, semantic system or speech output lexicon because, by definition, unfamiliar words and nonwords do not look familiar, convey no meaning to the reader, and their pronunciations have not (yet) been stored away.

What, then, is the procedure that allows a reader to read aloud an unfamiliar string of letters? In Fig. 3.1, the procedure is implied by the connection between the visual analysis system to the phoneme level. The visual analysis system identifies letters and notes their positions, while the phoneme level represents individual speech sounds, even when the letters are part of an unfamiliar word or nonword. By connecting the two we allow letters (and letter groups) to activate the sounds with which they are most typically associated in English. This is the procedure that allows a reader to take a nonword like TEP, identify its component letters (T1, E2, P3) and convert each into the phoneme it characteristically represents (in English words with regular spellings) to produce "tep". It would also allow the reader who has never seen TIP written down before, but knows the spoken word, to convert TIP from print to sound and then identify the word.

The procedure for connecting letters to sounds must do more than associate individual letter identities with individual phonemes. The subtleties of English spelling demand that it must also be sensitive to the grouping of letters. For example, it must know that PH is typically pronounced "f" and that the E at the end of MAPE will modify the pronunciation of the central vowel as it does in words such as MADE and MATE (cf. MAP, MAD and MAT).

This letter-to-sound procedure operates without regard to whether the letters it is converting to sounds occur in familiar words, unfamiliar words or nonwords, and hence is sometimes referred to as the "non-lexical procedure" (or "non-lexical route"). Because it operates on units smaller than words (letters and letter groups), it sometimes goes under the alternative name of the "sublexical procedure" (or "sublexical route"). Teachers know it as phonic reading skill.

Independence of the Lexical and Sublexical Procedures

Figure 3.1 represents the lexical procedures that convert print to sound for familiar words (reading via meaning and the non-semantic route) as largely separate from the sublexical procedure that pronounces unfamiliar words and nonwords. In reality, the lexical and sublexical procedures may not be quite so distinct. Kay and Marcel (1981) had subjects read aloud nonwords that were preceded by familiar words. The experimental manipulation of importance for the present argument involved nonwords such as COTH and GAID. The regular pronunciation of COTH rhymes with MOTH and the regular pronunciation of GAID rhymes with PAID. Kay and Marcel found that if COTH and GAID were preceded by MOTH and PAID respectively, then they were duly assigned their regular pronunciations. But if the irregular word BOTH preceded COTH and the irregular word SAID preceded GAID, then at least some subjects pronounced the nonwords so as to rhyme with the irregular words they followed. If the pronunciation given to an unfamiliar word or nonword can be biased by recent experience with familiar words, then the lexical and sublexical procedures must interact more than the layout of Fig. 3.1 might suggest.

Some current models refuse to acknowledge any distinction between sublexical and lexical (non-semantic) reading procedures (e.g. Seidenberg & McClelland, 1989; Shallice & Warrington, 1980). These models suggest that readers learn associations between print and sound at a variety of levels ranging from correspondences between individual letters and phonemes, through correspondences involving letter groups and syllables, to associations between print and sound at the level of whole words.

There are almost certainly times when word-level knowledge may be brought to bear upon the task of reading an unfamiliar word. Imagine, for example, that an unfamiliar word being read for the first time is a compound noun formed from two familiar words (e.g. SPARROWHAWK or SWALLOWTAIL). It seems highly unlikely that a skilled reader will break these right down into their component letters in order to read them aloud, and much more likely that he or she will pronounce them by accessing the pronunciations of their component words as a whole and simply running them together. Other long words encountered for the first time (e.g. KISHKEMUNASEE) do not lend themselves so readily to this procedure and will need to be read more analytically, making more use of small-scale letter–sound correspondences.

Regularity Effects in Reading Aloud

Whether the sublexical procedure is a separate route or just fine-grain associations within a larger system, there is nothing to stop that procedure contributing to the task of reading familiar words aloud, even though its main purpose in life is to allow visually unfamiliar words to be read. If the sublexical procedure is active when a word with a regular spelling is being read, then it should generate a pronunciation which agrees with that produced by the lexical procedure (i.e. the pronunciation emanating from the speech output lexicon). But when the word being read has an irregular spelling, the sublexical route will tend to regularise it and so produce an incorrect and conflicting pronunciation. Thus, if the familiar word being read is PINT, the sublexical procedure may generate a pronunciation to rhyme with HINT, DINT and MINT rather than the correct pronunciation which, because PINT is an irregular word, can only be accessed from the speech output lexicon. The extra time needed to resolve the conflict between rival pronunciations of irregular words could explain the slower naming speeds for irregular words noted in Chapter 2. Because the conflict arises in the process of settling upon a pronunciation, rather than in initial visual recognition or semantic access, regularity of spelling–sound correspondence should affect naming speed but not the time required to make a lexical decision response, which is the pattern of data that is observed.

With a few more plausible assumptions we can go on to explain why the regular–irregular word difference should be greater for low-frequency words than for high-frequency words. Suppose that the sublexical procedure tends to be rather slow, involving as it does the dissection of letter strings into elements that are then converted into phonemes which must be blended to create the final pronunciation. Suppose also that the speed with which the non-semantic, whole-word route involving visual input lexicon to speech output lexicon connections depends on the frequency with which a reader has encountered a given word in the past (because high-frequency words have lower thresholds or stronger connections). The whole-word route may deliver the pronunciation of a high-frequency, irregular word before the sublexical route has a chance to assemble a conflicting pronunciation, but the whole-word retrieval of the pronunciation of a low-frequency irregular word may tend to coincide with the arrival at the phoneme level of a contrasting, regularised pronunciation emanating from the sublexical route. We should then expect to see the reported interaction between frequency and regularity whereby low-frequency irregular words take longer to read aloud than low-frequency regular words, but no such difference exists between reading speeds for high-frequency regular and irregular words.

THE ROLE OF SOUND IN ACCESSING THE MEANINGS OF FAMILIAR WORDS

It is much easier to study reading aloud than reading comprehension. Scanning the literature on skilled reading, one could be forgiven for thinking that the goal of reading is to turn print into speech. Of course, it is not: the goal of reading is to understand (perhaps even to enjoy) a piece of text.

In Fig. 3.1 the only way into the semantic system is via the visual input lexicon. This allows familiar written words to access their meanings without any intervention of the sound-forms of those words. This notion of direct access to meanings from written word-forms has been hotly debated. Some theorists believe that it is the dominant procedure and that the sound-forms of familiar words play little or no part in the process of accessing their meanings (e.g. Coltheart, 1978; Rumelhart & Siple, 1974). At the other extreme stand theorists who have suggested that accessing meanings via sound is the normal procedure (e.g. Gough, 1972).

After a number of years during which this particular debate had been fairly quiet, Van Orden and his colleagues reawakened the issue with a series of papers reporting experiments whose results seem to imply a major role for sound in accessing the meanings of familiar words (Van Orden, 1987; Van Orden, Johnston, & Hale,1988; Van Orden, Pennington, & Stone, 1990). Their basic experimental paradigm involves subjects seeing the name of a semantic category (e.g. *A type of fruit*), followed by a target word which could call for a Yes response (e.g. PEAR) or a No response (e.g. POUR). Responding might involve pressing one of two keys as quickly as possible. What interested Van Orden and colleagues is what happened if a word which should elicit a No response was the homophone of a word that would elicit a Yes response (e.g. *A type of fruit*–PAIR). What they found is that subjects made a lot of "false positive" errors under those conditions, pressing the Yes key instead of the No key. These errors indicate that the subjects were being misled by the sounds of the target words and that sounds were being activated as part of the quest for meaning.

This effect occurs when subjects are under pressure to respond rapidly. The first point to note is that a skilled reader would make far fewer of these errors if given more time to decide whether a PAIR is a fruit or not. A skilled reader's ability to respond correctly to homophones when not under time pressure (and to respond correctly most of the time even when under pressure) proves that meanings are not accessed *only* via sound. If they were, then a reader would have no way of knowing which of PEAR and PAIR was a fruit and which was two of a kind. Jared and Seidenberg (1991) showed that the homophone effect only held strongly for lower frequency homophones. Their subjects sometimes mistakenly pressed the Yes button when asked if WAIL was a sea mammal but were less prone to error when asked if SUN was a male relative or MEET was food.

For the sounds of words to play *any* part in accessing their meanings requires some modification of Fig. 3.1. One possible explanation begins with the non-semantic route from the visual input lexicon to the speech output lexicon depositing a spoken word-form in the phoneme level. That sound-form might then be spoken internally as "inner speech". If the task is to decide if WAIL is a sea mammal, the sound-form being spoken internally would sound right, and might tend to elicit a Yes response, even though the written word-form would be activating a different meaning. An alternative but similar explanation might propose that, like many of the connections in Fig. 3.1, the connection between the semantic system and the speech output lexicon is bi-directional. WAIL would then activate its correct meaning via the links between the visual input lexicon and the semantic system, and its sound via the links between the visual input lexicon and the speech output lexicon, but activation passing up from the speech output lexicon to the semantic system could also cause the meaning of WHALE to be activated. Either way, Jared and Seidenberg's (1991) result shows that activating meaning via sound only interferes with activating meaning direct from print when the word being processed is a low-frequency word whose processing will be generally slower than that of a high-frequency word.

The position adopted in this book will be that when a skilled reader fixates a very familiar word, access to its meaning occurs directly from print, with the sound of the word having only a minor role. When a skilled reader fixates a somewhat less familiar word, but one that has nevertheless been encountered before, then access to meaning directly from print and indirectly via the sound of the word may occur more or less simultaneously and in parallel. When the word has never been seen before, but has been heard before, then access to meaning can *only* occur via sound (though in this case the sound-form is generated piecemeal using the sublexical procedure). Figure 3.1 is doubtless some way from being a correct and true model of word recognition in reading, but it seems to have some merits, and it will be used as the basis for analysing disorders of word recognition in the next chapter.

NOTES

1. Referred to in the first edition of *Reading, Writing and Dyslexia* as the "visual word recognition system".
2. Referred to in the first edition of *Reading, Writing and Dyslexia* as the "phonemic word production system".
3. Referred to in the first edition of *Reading, Writing, and Dyslexia* as the "phonemic buffer".

FURTHER READING

Besner, D. & Humphreys, G.W. (Eds.). (1991). *Basic processes in reading: Visual word recognition.* Hillsdale, NJ: Lawrence Erlbaum Associates Inc.

Henderson, L. (1982). *Orthography and word recognition in reading.* London: Academic Press.

Humphreys, G.W. & Bruce, V. (1989). *Visual cognition: Computational, experimental and neuropsychological perspectives.* Hove: Lawrence Erlbaum Associates Ltd.

Patterson, K. & Coltheart, V. (1987). Phonological processes in reading: A tutorial review. In M. Coltheart (Ed.), *Attention and performance XII: The psychology of reading.* Hove: Lawrence Erlbaum Associates Ltd.

Rayner, K. & Pollatsek, A. (1989). *The psychology of reading.* Englewood Cliffs, NJ: Prentice-Hall.

CHAPTER FOUR

The Acquired Dyslexias

The brain is the organ of the mind. It is also an organ of the body and, as such, is susceptible to injury and illness. The most common cause of injury to the brain is a stroke; that is, a disruption of the blood supply to a part of the brain which may be caused by the bursting of an artery (haemorrhage) or the blockage of an artery by a blood clot. Working in France in the 1860s, Paul Broca showed that, in right-handed people, language problems tend to occur after damage to the left rather than the right half of the brain. It is the left half, or hemisphere, of the brain which in most people is primarily responsible for language abilities, including the skills of reading and writing.

Disorders affecting the comprehension or production of spoken language which occur as a consequence of brain injury are known as aphasias. There are many different types of aphasia, depending upon just what aspects of speech processing have been impaired (Ellis & Young, 1988; McCarthy & Warrington, 1990). Aphasic patients often experience reading difficulties which are part and parcel of their more general language impairments. On other occasions, reading problems are the predominant symptom, or cannot be explained solely by reference to the broader aphasia. In either case, we would talk about the patient suffering from an "acquired dyslexia". Acquired dyslexia was studied in the late nineteenth century by neurologists such as Carl Wernicke, but most of the research on acquired dyslexias has been done since the mid-1970s. Cognitive psychology, which is the study of normal mental processes such as perception, memory, language and reading, came together at that point with neuropsychology, which is the study of the human brain and its functions, to create cognitive neuropsychology, the study of disorders of cognitive function that arise as a consequence of brain injury. When cognitive neuropsychologists investigate acquired dyslexia, their approach is not so much to ask which part of the brain is damaged in which form of reading disorder, but to ask which part or parts of the normal reading process have been damaged or lost. That is, they seek to explain different patterns of reading breakdown by reference to models of the normal, skilled reading process such as that presented in Fig. 3.1.

Such cognitive models inccrporate a number of different processes ranging from letter identification and visual word recognition, to semantic comprehension and phonological appreciation of the sound-forms of words. If brain injury can affect each of those aspects of reading, damaging certain aspects in one patient and other aspects in another, then we should expect to see a variety of qualitatively different forms of acquired dyslexia, which we do. We might also expect to be able to explain each form of acquired dyslexia by giving an account of which aspects of normal skilled reading have been impaired (and how), and which remain more or less intact. That, broadly speaking, is the goal of the cognitive neuropsychological study of acquired dyslexia.

But cognitive neuropsychologists also want to be able to use data from patients to test and develop theories of normal skilled reading. They want data from patients to be regarded as being on a par with data from laboratory experiments with normal subjects. For example, a cognitive neuropsychologist might assert that it would not be possible to observe a particular pattern of acquired reading disorder if the normal reading system were organised in one way, but could be accounted for if the normal system were organised in another, different way. Examples of this mode of argument will be presented in this chapter. Virtually all of the work done on acquired dyslexia has concentrated on patients' ability to read single words, so it is models of word recognition rather than theories of sentence or text processing that have been considered relevant, and that studies of acquired dyslexia have been directed towards.

Shallice and Warrington (1980) introduced a useful distinction between peripheral and central acquired dyslexias that we shall follow here. In terms of the model presented in Fig. 3.1, peripheral dyslexias are disorders in which the visual analysis system is damaged, resulting in a range of conditions in which the perception of letters in words is impaired. The central dyslexias are a collection of disorders in which processes beyond the visual analysis system are damaged, resulting in difficulties affecting the comprehension and/or pronunciation of written words.

PERIPHERAL DYSLEXIAS

Neglect Dyslexia

Ellis, Flude, and Young (1987) reported the case of patient V.B. who, unlike most acquired dyslexics, was not aphasic—her capacity to speak and to understand the speech of others was unimpaired by the stroke she had experienced. This was because V.B.'s stroke had affected the right side of her brain rather than the left side which, as we have seen, is for most people the side which controls language use. Nevertheless, V.B. had problems with reading. When she was trying to read passages of text she would often make no attempt to read the first few words of each line. When shown single words, she made errors affecting the first letter or two. For example, she misread NUN as "run", YELLOW as "pillow", CLOVE as "love" and HADDOCK as "paddock". If V.B. was asked to read a word and also explain what it meant, the definition she gave always matched the error she made. Thus, she misread RICE as "price" and defined it as "how much for a paper or something in a shop", misread LIQUID as "squid" and said it was "a kind of sea creature", and misread CLOVER as "lover", adding, "partner, or someone you have an affair with; a sweetheart".

V.B.'s problem was definitely visual in nature. Her identification of words spelled aloud to her was excellent, and if a passage of text was rotated clockwise through 90° so that the lines ran from top to bottom rather than from left to right, her performance improved considerably. The majority of her errors involved replacing rather than simply deleting the initial letters of words. This was true even when deleting the first letter or two left a real word. Thus she misread FABLE as "table" rather than "able", and BEAT as "heat" rather than "eat". That is, even when she got the first letters of a word wrong, she seemed in some way to know that there were letters there.

One account of this form of neglect dyslexia asserts that the problem arises from a failure to attend to the left side of words. Riddoch, Humphreys, Cleton, and Fery (1991) sought to test this by examining the effect of deliberately drawing a patient's attention to the left sides of words. They described a patient, J.B., with a neglect dyslexia similar to V.B.'s. Examples of J.B.'s errors are GROSS misread as "cross" and BOUGH as "slough". Riddoch et al. tested the attentional theory by placing a hash sign (#) to the left of words and instructing J.B. to locate the hash before attempting to read each word aloud. Performance improved relative to his reading of the same words without hashes, lending support to the attentional theory.

The attentional problem experienced by V.B., J.B. and other patients like them affects their ability to identify the beginning letters of words though they retain some awareness of the presence of letters in those initial positions. Somewhat different varieties of neglect dyslexia requiring some-what different explanations are reviewed by Ellis, Young, and Flude (1993).

Attentional Dyslexia

Given the fact that we have just ascribed neglect dyslexia to a disorder of attention, it is more than a little confusing to find the next variety of acquired dyslexia labelled "attentional dyslexia". Shallice and Warrington (1977) described two acquired dyslexic patients who were reasonably good at reading words presented singly and who could name single letters almost perfectly. These patients" problems arose when there were several letters in a row or several words on the page. They then began to make errors. Where words were concerned, the errors they made were very similar to errors that can be observed in normal skilled readers if groups of words are presented very briefly. Under those circumstances, letters may "migrate" from one word to another, so that a subject shown GLOVE and SPADE may report having seen "GLADE" (Allport, 1977; Mozer, 1983). The difference between these normal readers and Shallice and Warrington's (1977) patients is that the patients made errors even when given unlimited time to read the words. Shallice and Warrington suggest that an atten-tional process is required to focus upon a letter or word that is being identified and to ensure that one is not flooded with information from else-where in the visual world. This attentional process is deficient in atten-tional dyslexia and is presumably prevented from functioning properly in normal readers when groups of words are displayed for very brief intervals.

Letter-by-letter Reading

Some patients, faced with a written word, will work their way laboriously through it, identifying the letters one at a time before trying to say what the word is. Such patients are known as "letter-by-letter readers" (Patterson & Kay, 1982; Warrington & Shallice, 1980). It is important to appreciate that these patients are not reading phonically: they convert letters into their names (Aitch, Vee) not their sounds ("huh", "vuh"). Although their word recognition is slow and error-prone, they read irregular words ("Y, A, C, H, T . . . yacht") as successfully as regular words ("S, H, I, P . . . ship").

Because they identify one letter at a time, the longer a word is, the longer they take to identify it. This is a hallmark of letter-by-letter reading, even in patients who employ the strategy without naming the letters aloud. The speed with which skilled readers can identify familiar words shows only a very small effect of the number of letters in a word, because the visual analysis system of skilled readers can identify the component letters of a word simultaneously, and can transmit those letters "in parallel" to the visual input lexicon. Letter-by-letter readers, in contrast, are reduced to a serial, one-letter-at-a-time identification process (though precisely how they identify words, and what role letter names play in identification, is still unclear).

CENTRAL DYSLEXIAS

Non-semantic Reading

Schwartz, Marin, and Saffran (1979) and Schwartz, Saffran, and Marin (1980) describe a 62-year-old woman, W.L.P., who was suffering from a progressive dementia, including a generalised loss of memory. At one stage in her illness, W.L.P. was quite unable to match written animal names against their appropriate pictures. When presented with 20 low-frequency animal names such as hyena, leopard and llama, together with some names of body parts and some colour names, she could only sort out 7 of the 20 animal names as referring to animals at all. Nevertheless, she managed to read aloud 18 of the 20 animal names, including the three mentioned above, and made only minor errors on the other two. In general, W.L.P. displayed a remarkable capacity to read words aloud despite showing very little evidence of understanding many of them, and despite being quite unable to use them in her own limited spontaneous speech. Nevertheless, until the final stages of her illness, she could read aloud both regular and irregular words and could also read nonwords aloud.

As far as one can tell, W.L.P. was not reading via meanings. She could read nonwords, so her sublexical letter–sound conversion procedures were preserved, but she could also read irregular words aloud correctly, implying preservation of whole-word reading via the lexicons. Yet comprehension of written words was very poor. In terms of Fig. 3.1, we would say that W.L.P. had an impaired semantic system but was still able to read words aloud using the connections between the visual input lexicon and the speech output lexicon. Indeed, the existence of patients like W.L.P. might be taken as evidence for the existence of such a non-semantic but lexical reading procedure. W.L.P.'s ability to read nonwords implies that the connections between the visual analysis system and the phoneme level were also preserved.

Surface Dyslexia

It is normal in reviews of this kind to present the symptoms of a particular kind of disorder and then discuss the interpretation, but for this and the next variety of acquired dyslexia it is easier to take the reverse approach— to present the interpretation and then work back to the symptoms.

The term "surface dyslexia" was coined by John Marshall and Freda Newcombe in their seminal paper, "Patterns of paralexia: A psycholinguistic approach", published in 1973. Surface dyslexics show a high reliance on the sublexical procedure in reading aloud; that is, on letter–sound conversion using the route connecting the visual analysis system to the phoneme level. They treat once-familiar words as if they were unfamiliar, breaking them down into their component letters and letter groups, converting each into phonemes and pronouncing the resulting sound sequence. This works reasonably well for regular words because they are by definition the words whose letter–sound relations match the normal correspondences of English. Surface dyslexics are, however, prone to misread irregular words, pronouncing them as if they were regular. Thus ISLAND becomes "izland", SUGAR becomes "sudger" and BROAD becomes "brode".

Better reading aloud of regular than irregular words with regularisation errors to irregular words are the hallmarks of surface dyslexia (Patterson, Marshall, & Coltheart, 1985). We shall encounter them again when we come to look at the reading profiles of normal young children and some developmental dyslexics. According to Fig. 3.1, whole-word reading requires words to be recognised by the visual input lexicon and their pronunciations to be retrieved from the speech output lexicon. Connection between the two lexicons may be either direct or via the semantic system. It is clear that damage at more than one location could force the use of the sublexical procedure for reading aloud; for example, damage to the visual input lexicon or damage to the speech output lexicon. Although damage at these different loci will all result in phonological reading of the sort shown by surface dyslexics, it should be possible to distinguish them in other ways. For example, a patient who is surface dyslexic because of damage to the visual input lexicon will not know what a word she cannot pronounce correctly means, whereas a patient who is surface dyslexic because of damage to the speech output lexicon should still know what a mispronounced word means. Evidence that these different sub-types of surface dyslexia may exist is discussed in Ellis and Young (1988).

Phonological Dyslexia

Phonological dyslexia is in many ways the mirror image of surface dyslexia. The sublexical procedure that mediates much of the reading performance of a surface dyslexic is precisely the procedure that is impaired in phonological dyslexia. The result is a mild form of acquired dyslexia, which could easily be missed if one were not on the look out for it, a fact which may explain why it has only been noticed and reported relatively recently.

Phonological dyslexics are no longer able to make effective use of the sublexical reading procedure represented in Fig. 3.1 by the connection between the visual analysis system and the phoneme level. As a result, they are virtually unable to read unfamiliar words or invented nonwords aloud. Familiar words, in contrast, can be read reasonably successfully. Patient W.B. reported by Funnell (1983) read 93 of a set of 100 common nouns correctly but could manage only 2 of 20 simple nonwords. Often the best she could do was to read a nonword as a similar-looking familiar word (e.g. reading COBE as "comb", PLOON as "spoon" and FUDE as "fudge"). These errors are known as "lexicalisations". The relative preservation of word reading suggests (among other things) a preservation of the visual input lexicon. W.B. seemed to be able to make a response to a nonword by allowing its sequence of letters to activate the closest recognition unit in the visual input lexicon.

Phonological dyslexia may seem an abstruse form of reading disorder (patients with acquired dyslexia who can read real words quite well), but it is of theoretical interest for at least two reasons. One is the "double dissociation" it forms with surface dyslexia. Phonological dyslexics read on a whole-word basis and are severely impaired at the sort of sublexical processing required to read unfamiliar words and nonwords aloud. Surface dyslexics, in contrast, rely heavily on sublexical processing and have impaired whole-word recognition processes. So phonological dyslexics have reasonably intact whole-word recognition but impaired sublexical procedures, whereas surface dyslexics show the opposite pattern. Cognitive neuropsychologists interpret such "double dissociations" as indicating that whole-word and sublexical reading are mediated by cognitive processes (modules) that are at least to some degree separate within the mind and brain. That is, they interpret the contrast between phonological and surface dyslexia as supporting the separation in Fig. 3.1 of sublexical letter–sound conversion procedures mediated by connections between the visual analysis system and the phoneme level from whole-word recognition mediated by the visual input lexicon.

The second reason why acquired phonological dyslexia is of interest is that many of the children diagnosed as having developmental dyslexia present with symptoms very like those of acquired phonological dyslexia, so much so that it has become quite common for psychologists to talk about "developmental phonological dyslexia". We shall discuss possible parallels between developmental and acquired dyslexia, and some reasons for caution, in Chapter 8.

Deep Dyslexia

Imagine yourself seated at a table in a hospital room. Opposite you is a patient who has suffered a stroke but who is alert and interested. You have brought along a pack of plain cards each of which has a single word written on it. You hold up a card bearing the word APE. "Can you read this word aloud for me?" you ask. "Certainly", replies the patient, "that's monkey". The next card you hold up bears the word SOUL, which the patient reads as "soup". He then goes on to read BABY correctly, LOVELY as "loving", HIS as "in", FOREST as "trees", WINDOW correctly, BOAP as "don't know", CHANCE as "don't know", SYMPATHY as "orchestra", SIGNAL as "single", QUITE as "perhaps", BELIEF as "pray", WAS as "one of those little words—don't know", WHEN as "chick" and BUILDING as "builder". If this did indeed happen to you, then you would know you were sitting opposite a patient with "deep dyslexia" (Coltheart, Patterson, & Marshall, 1987).

Deep dyslexics find words like BABY, CHURCH or TABLE, which have concrete, imageable referents, easier to read than abstract words like BELIEF, TRUTH or JUSTICE. Like phonological dyslexics, deep dyslexics also find unfamiliar words and nonwords virtually impossible to read aloud. Deep dyslexics also make several different types of reading error. First and most striking are the "semantic errors" such as misreading APE as "monkey", FOREST as "trees" or BELIEF as "pray". Secondly, there are visual errors (e.g. reading SOUL as "soup" or SIGNAL as "single"). A third type of error appears to be a combination of a visual error followed by a semantic error. For example, it is assumed that the patient who misread SYMPATHY as "orchestra" had made a visual error (misreading SYMPATHY as SYMPHONY, and had followed that with a semantic error to convert SYMPHONY into "orchestra"). Similarly, the patient who misread WHEN as "chick" is presumed to have combined a visual error (WHEN to HEN), followed by a semantic error (HEN to "chick").

LOVELY misread as "loving" and BUILDER as "building" are placed in a separate category of "derivational errors", though we may note that the target and error words are both visually and semantically related in these cases. Finally, HIS misread as "in" or QUITE as "perhaps" are termed "function word substitutions". It seems surprising that deep dyslexics have such difficulty with what are some of the most common words in the language, but the explanation may lie in the fact that although they are common words, the meanings of function words like IN, QUITE and PERHAPS are abstract and hard to visualise. It may be the abstractness of function words that makes them hard for deep dyslexics. Note, though, that the errors made to function words usually involve substituting another function word, so the patient seems to know at some level what *sort* of word he or she is being asked to read.

Although patients with symptoms like those of deep dyslexia have been reported from time to time over the years (Marshall & Newcombe, 1980), the first full descriptions were provided by Marshall and Newcombe in 1966 and again in the same 1973 paper in which surface dyslexia was reported. Marshall and Newcombe adopted the same approach to explaining deep dyslexia as they took to explaining surface dyslexia; that is, trying to explain the disorder in terms of impairment to components of a model of normal reading. The semantic errors and the imageability effect (better reading of concrete than abstract nouns and, perhaps, the problem with function words) suggest two things. One is that deep dyslexics attempt to read via the semantic system; the second is that there is damage in or around that system. At least some deep dyslexics are able to recognise abstract words as words in a lexical decision task even though they cannot read them aloud (Patterson, 1979). This suggests that in these patients the visual input lexicon continues to function, but the direct connections between the visual input lexicon and the speech output lexicon (which, if present, could support non-semantic reading) must be lost.

The almost complete inability of deep dyslexics to read nonwords aloud suggests that they have also lost the capacity for sublexical letter–sound conversion; that is, the connections between the visual analysis system and the phoneme level are gone. This may be a necessary condition for semantic errors to occur in any numbers, because even a little phonic skill might prevent a patient from misreading FOREST as "trees" (because the patient would know that the correct pronunciation should start with an "f" sound).

Any explanation of deep dyslexia in terms of damage to the normal reading process will have to postulate several different impairments. The appropriateness of such accounts of deep dyslexia has, however, been challenged by Coltheart (1980; 1983). He argues that in deep dyslexia we are not seeing the effects of loss of some aspects of the normal, left hemisphere reading system. Instead, Coltheart argues that in deep dyslexics most of the left hemisphere reading processes have been completely destroyed and the residual reading abilities are mediated by the patient's *right* hemisphere, which is normally considered "non-verbal" but which may play host to certain limited language skills, at least in some people. Some support for this hypothesis has come in the form of a report by Patterson, Vargha-Khadem, and Polkey (1989) of the case of a 17-year-old girl, N.I. After an apparently normal childhood, N.I. became severely epileptic with almost continuous seizures and a progressive degeneration of the left cerebral hemisphere, which would almost certainly have proved fatal had the diseased hemisphere not been removed in its entirety. After a period of recovery, N.I. was shown to have retained some reading capacity, but her residual reading abilities showed strong similarities to those of deep dyslexic patients. N.I. was significantly better at reading concrete than abstract nouns, made semantic errors (e.g. misreading ARM as "finger") and visual errors (e.g. misreading BUSH as "brush"), and was very poor at reading nonwords.

The report of N.I.'s deep dyslexic reading after surgical removal of the left hemisphere clearly supports the right hemisphere hypothesis of deep dyslexia, but the rival view that deep dyslexia can, at least sometimes, reflect the residual capabilities of a damaged left hemisphere, still has its adherents. We should note, though, that if the right hemisphere hypothesis proves to be correct, then studying deep dyslexia may not teach us much about normal reading processes. At best, we might learn about the properties of a secondary system whose contribution, if any, to normal reading we would then have to work out.

FURTHER READING

Coltheart, M., Patterson, K.E., & Marshall, J.C. (Eds.). (1987). *Deep dyslexia* (2nd ed.). London: Routledge and Kegan Paul.

Ellis, A.W. & Young, A.W. (1988). *Human cognitive neuropsychology.* Hove: Lawrence Erlbaum Associates Ltd.

McCarthy, R.A. & Warrington, E.K. (1990). *Cognitive neuropsychology: A clinical introduction.* London: Academic Press.

Patterson, K.E., Coltheart, M., & Marshall, J.C. (Eds.). (1985). *Surface dyslexia: Neuropsychological and cognitive studies of phonological reading.* Hove: Lawrence Erlbaum Associates Ltd.

Shallice, T. (1988). *From neuropsychology to mental structure.* Cambridge: Cambridge University Press.

CHAPTER FIVE

Words in Combinations

So far, we have concentrated on how skilled readers recognise written words, and on how those recognition processes can be disturbed in patients with acquired dyslexia. We have briefly mentioned that the context in which a word occurs affects the ease with which it can be recognised, but that is about as far as we have gone towards acknowledging the fact that reading is normally something that involves sentences, paragraphs, articles, chapters and books. It is now time to redress the balance a little.

COMPREHENDING TEXT

Memory for "Gist"

When psychologists have studied long-term memory for things read or heard, they have often tended to ask subjects to remember the precise wording of something, where the "something" in question may be a list of words or a passage of text (Baddeley, 1990; Ebbinghaus, 1885). But if you were to ask someone who is not a subject in a psychology experiment to recall a book or article they read last week, they would never dream of attempting to recall the thing verbatim (and you would think them most odd if they did). What your informant would do naturally is attempt to recall the "gist" of the original—its plot or the ideas it contained. Only a few of the actual words of the original may reappear in the recall.

The French psychologist Alfred Binet is best remembered nowadays as the creator of one of the first "intelligence" tests for children, but as part of his broader research into child development he studied children's recall of passages of text. He showed that when children recall passages they have read, even after a short interval, they will often replace words from the original with others which have similar meanings. Binet and Henri (1894) argued that this phenomenon "indicates the disappearance of verbal memory and the retention of the memory for ideas". The recall of a sentence immediately after reading or hearing it may reproduce the wording of the original quite well, but if any significant interval of time is allowed to pass, then only the gist may remain.

Everyone has an intuitive understanding of what is meant by "gist", but how should we define and study it? That problem has taxed many psychologists, though it is questionable whether a decent answer has yet been given. One answer that has received some support is that the gist of a piece of text lies in the *propositions* it contains. A proposition is a unit of meaning which can be either true or false. The same proposition can be expressed in different languages or in different ways in the same language (e.g. *The brown monkey is in the tree–Le singe brun est dans l'arbre; In the tree there is a brown monkey–Dans l'arbre c'est un singe brun*). A sentence will often contain a number of propositions. Thus, all the variants of the sentence *The brown monkey is in the tree* contain the same two propositions—*The monkey is in the tree* and *The monkey is brown*.

Kintsch and van Dijk (1978) and van Dijk and Kintsch (1983) developed an influential theory of comprehension in which propositions play a crucial role. The theory is complex and we can do no more than give a feel for it here. In Kintsch and van Dijk's theory, comprehension involves first of all extracting the propositions from a sentence or passage. Those propositions are then combined to form a structured, coherent representation which captures the way the propositions relate one to another. Kintsch and Keenan (1973) found that if two sentences or paragraphs have the same number of words, the one containing more propositions will take longer to read. This has been interpreted as showing that the extraction of propositions from text is a real and time-consuming process.

Once a structured representation has been created, it is then linked to existing knowledge in long-term memory, thereby expanding and adding to that knowledge. The theory has spawned a great deal of research, much of which has proved supportive. It has been criticised for lacking detail in certain areas, and it would never claim to capture all there is to say about the understanding of discourse (Rayner & Pollatsek, 1989). Nevertheless, Kintsch and van Dijk's theory gives one some idea of how the concept of "gist" may be made more concrete, and how testable theories of comprehension might be developed.

Schemas

We need to introduce another somewhat technical term at this juncture, and that is the term "schema". Psychologists use the word "schema" to describe a person's organised and integrated knowledge about a particular topic (for example, knowledge of what goes on in a restaurant or at the dentist that has been built up as a result of pleasant or painful experience).

Bartlett (1932) is generally credited with introducing the schema concept into psychology. Bartlett studied memory in a variety of situations and forms, including memory for text. One of his demonstrations involved asking subjects to re-tell the same story repeatedly over a period of time. Bartlett showed that an initially rather incoherent story will be made more intelligible in the re-telling, with irrelevant details being "levelled out", relevant details "sharpened", and unexplained features of the original "rationalised". Zangwill (1939) showed that after a re-telling or two, subjects are unable to distinguish elements of the original from elements they introduced themselves, while Davis and Sinha (1950) demonstrated how story elements fuse with things picked up from accompanying pictures in such a way that the subject soon has difficulty recalling what came from which source.

Demonstrations that comprehension and recall of text are influenced by knowledge activated at the time are taken as evidence for the relevance of the schema concept to understanding reading comprehension. For example, Sulin and Dooling (1974) created a passage about a politician who became a dictator and was eventually responsible for his country's downfall. In fact, there were two versions of the passage, one in which the dictator was given the fictitious name of Gerald Martin and one in which he was called Adolf Hitler. Memory for the text was tested either after 5 min or after a week. The test took the form of presenting the subjects with a set of sentences, half of which were "old" sentences from the original passage, while the other half were "new". The subjects had to indicate which of the sentences were "old" and which "new". The catch was that all the "new" sentences mentioned things that people know to be true of Adolf Hitler but would have no particular reason to attribute to Gerald Martin (e.g. *He hated Jews particularly and so persecuted them*). After just 5 min, all of the subjects were quite good at distinguishing old from new sentences, and even after a week the "Gerald Martin" subjects performed quite well. But for the "Adolf Hitler" subjects, the new information gleaned from the passage had blended after a week with their general knowledge to the point where they could no longer distinguish "old" sentences extracted from the passage from "new" sentences containing things they knew to be true of the Führer.

Sulin and Dooling's effect depends on the name "Adolf Hitler" activating relevant schemata at the time of reading the passage. But performance can also be affected by activating relevant schemata at the time of recall. Anderson and Pichert (1978) devised a story in which two boys played truant from school and spent the day in one of their houses. The house was nice but old, having a leaky roof and a damp basement. The parents who owned the house were well off, so the house boasted fancy appliances, expensive bikes, a collection of rare coins, and so on. Half the subjects in the experiment were asked to read the passage from the point of view of a prospective home-buyer; the other half from the point of view of a prospective burglar. After reading the story, the subjects were asked to write down as much of it as they could. The "home-buyers" tended to remember the condition of the roof and cellar more than the contents, while the "burglars" showed the opposite pattern.

After a short delay, all of the subjects were asked to make a second attempt to recall the story. Half retained their original roles, but the other half swapped from being burglars to home-buyers, or vice versa. People who had previously been burglars, recalling the house contents but forgetting the state of the fabric of the building, now began to remember the leaking roof and the damp cellar. Similarly, people who had previously been home-buyers, recalling the state of the building but forgetting the house contents, now began to remember the appliances, bikes and coins. The subjects had encoded all the information in the story in memory when the passage was read, but the strength of the schemata active at first recall prevented irrelevant information from being recollected. But when the perspective changed and the schemata changed, and the nature of what was relevant changed, so previously irrelevant facts sprang to mind.

Inference and Elaboration

Reading, then, is an active process in which the reader brings a lifetime of experience (in the form of schemata) to the text and uses that experience to interpret and elaborate upon its contents. Writers rely on readers to make the inferences that allow the writer to avoid having to spell everything out in painful detail. For example, if you read *John was having stomach pains. Mary got out the telephone book*, you make at least two inferences (that John needed a doctor and that Mary got out the telephone book in order to look up the doctor's number). You would soon abandon a novel in which the writer wrote *John was having stomach pains. John needed a doctor. Mary got out the telephone book. She did that in order to look up the number*, and so on.

The business of making inferences seems effortless to a skilled reader, but Smith and Collins (1981) showed that passages which require the reader to draw even simple inferences take longer to read than passages in which everything is spelled out in detail so that no inferences are required. Sanford and Garrod (1981) experimented with passages in which the continuation of a passage implies that inferences the reader is likely to have drawn earlier are incorrect. Reading is slowed considerably to accommodate the reformulation that is required. For example, Sanford and Garrod recorded very long reading times on the last sentence of *John was on his way to school. He was worried about the maths lesson. He was afraid that he would be unable to control the class.* The reason for the lengthy reading times for the third sentence was assumed to be that readers had drawn the incorrect inference that John was a pupil and had work to do to realise that he was, in fact, a teacher.

Like information brought to a text in schemata, inferences drawn when reading a text become incorporated into memory. At a later date it may be impossible to distinguish inferences from things actually in the text. Johnson, Bransford, and Solomon (1973) presented subjects with two-sentence passages such as *John was trying to fix the bird house. He was pounding the nail when his father came to watch him and to help him do the work.* Not long after reading that passage, the subjects were likely to accept *John was using the hammer to fix the bird house when his father came out to watch him and to help him do the work* as being the thing they had read earlier. Not only is the latter version a single sentence when the original was two, but there is no explicit mention of a hammer in the original. Yet the hammer's presence had been inferred by the subjects when the original was read, so they were happy to accept it later as having been part of the original.

The fact that readers bring so much knowledge to bear on the task of comprehending text, and use that knowledge constantly to draw inferences, makes life hard for those whose ambition is to program computers to understand written language. Not only must the computer be equipped with the capacity to recognise words, activate individual word meanings, make use of sentence structure, and so on, it must also be armed with knowledge about the topics it must handle if it is to operate successfully. Schank and Abelson (1977) showed how a computer might be programmed with schematic knowledge about the sequences of actions that characterise situations such as eating in a restaurant. The computer's knowledge is organised into a *script* which has components like "entering", "ordering", "eating" and "leaving". Each component is broken down into smaller units, so that "ordering" includes "get menu", "look at menu", "choose food", and so on. This knowledge allows the computer to fill in gaps in stories (for example, inferring that if a diner orders food, he or she has already consulted a menu). The successes, problems and limitations of this approach are openly discussed by Schank (1982), along with ideas for advancing the work further. The great merit of this (and all other work within "artificial intelligence") is that trying to program computers to do things that humans do automatically and without thinking makes one aware of the sophistication of the mental machinery that underlies a cognitive skill like text comprehension. Computer modelling also disciplines the theorist to be clear, precise and detailed, acting as a valuable antidote to vague hand-waving (Johnson-Laird, 1988).

Aiding Comprehension by Activating Schemata

Schemata bring knowledge to text, knowledge that can help the reader to understand text which might otherwise be incomprehensible. Bransford and Johnson (1973) demonstrated this with sentences like *The notes were sour because the seams were split*, a sentence which is baffling until the relevant schema is triggered by a key word (in this case *Bagpipes*). The effect works with longer passages such as the following (taken from Dooling & Lachman, 1971):

> With hocked gems financing him, our hero bravely defied all scornful laughter that tried to prevent his scheme. Your eyes deceive you, he had said, an egg not a table correctly typifies this unexplored planet. Now three sturdy sisters sought proof, forging along sometimes through calm vastness, yet more often over turbulent peaks and valleys. Days became weeks and many doubters spread fearful rumours about the edge. At last, from nowhere, welcome winged creatures appeared, signifying monstrous success.

The key to activating the schema that will make that passage comprehensible is *Christopher Columbus*. If you look back to the passage now, with Christopher Columbus in mind, then you will be able to interpret the bit about the egg and the table as referring to the debate in the fifteenth century about the shape of the earth, the three sisters as Columbus's ships, the peaks and valleys as high seas, and so on.

Bransford and Johnson (1972) showed that if it is to be beneficial, the clue which helps readers bring the relevant knowledge base to bear must be provided *before* the text is read. Supplying the clue after a difficult text has been read is useless. This might seem to be at variance with the results of Anderson and Pichert's (1978) burglars and home-buyers experiment, but the passage used in that experiment was perfectly easy to comprehend and the differential effect of the two cues lay in the recall of its contents.

All the research we have just been reviewing was done within experimental cognitive psychology, but it fits well with similar work conducted in a more applied, educational setting. Ausubel (1960) required his subjects to read and remember the contents of a difficult passage dealing with the properties of carbon steel. Performance was greatly improved by a preliminary passage which activated more basic knowledge about metals and alloys—knowledge these particular subjects were presumed to have, but which possibly needed to be warmed up. Once warmed, it could be put to good use in helping to grasp and retain the experimental passage. Ausubel used the term "advance organisers" to refer to something which "bridge(s) the gap between what the reader already knows and what the reader needs to know before he/she can meaningfully learn the task at hand" (p. 148). Over two decades of research testifies to the value of enhancing comprehension by activating appropriate schemata through advance organisers, which may be a preliminary passage of text, but can be as simple as a helpful title or accompanying figure (Dole, Valencia, Greer, & Wardrop, 1991; Hartley & Davis, 1976; Moore & Readence, 1980). Of course, advance organisers only work if the knowledge is in memory in the first place: mention of the name Christopher Columbus will not help readers who know nothing about him to understand the passage reproduced above.

READING AND LISTENING

In trying to write about the comprehension of text, the writer encounters a problem, which is that researchers studying language comprehension tend to assume that the same mechanisms are responsible for comprehending both spoken and written language. Many of the oft-cited experiments on language comprehension happen to have used spoken sentences and passages as their materials rather than written ones. And yet it is typically assumed that conclusions about spoken language comprehension apply equally to the comprehension of written language.

Some evidence in support of this assumption comes from studies which have directly compared reading and listening comprehension in the same individuals. If the same processes are responsible for spoken and written language comprehension, then people who are good at the one should also be good at the other. Palmer, MacLeod, Hunt, and Davidson (1985) compared the scores of a group of college students on a test of listening comprehension with a composite score based on three tests of reading comprehension. The correlation between reading and listening scores was a high 0.82, and reading comprehension was almost perfectly predicted by listening comprehension scores. From this they conclude that "reading comprehension ability is indistinguishable from listening comprehension ability" (p. 59). The products of reading and listening comprehension also turn out to be very similar, both in terms of propositions recalled (Kintsch & Kozminsky, 1977) and ideas remembered (Smiley et al., 1977).

The language of written text often differs from the language of conversational speech in its style and complexity, but theories of language comprehension assume that comprehension skills acquired as a result of reading will thenceforth be available for listening, and vice versa. Curtis (1980) and Stanovich, Cunningham, and Freeman (1984) showed that as children's reading ability improves, listening comprehension improves in tandem. The converse should also be true: improving children's listening skills should have the effect of improving their reading comprehension.

LITERACY, TEXT AND MEMORY

Lengthy Verbatim Recall

We have noted the loss under natural conditions of verbatim details of the wording of text and the retention of the abstracted gist. But there are times when people *do* learn sizeable chunks of text "off by heart". It is no good, for example, an actor reciting the gist of Hamlet's soliloquy: the audience wants the words as Shakespeare wrote them, not an actor's paraphrase.

Humans are capable of prodigious feats of verbatim recall (for example, Islamic scholars have been known to learn all 6666 verses of the Koran word perfect). A commonly held but, it turns out, mistaken belief is that lengthy verbatim recall of stories, histories or religious epics can be observed in non-literate societies. This myth has been effectively exploded by Hunter (1984; 1985). Using data collected by anthropologists and linguists (e.g. Lord, 1960), Hunter was able to compare recitations of the "same" piece by different members of a non-literate society, or by the same person on different occasions. Either way, he was able to show that no two performances are ever identical. What non-literate singers and storytellers do is develop great skill in transforming detailed knowledge of the structure and facts of a narrative into verse "on the fly". The content of a tale may be faithfully reproduced time after time, but the wording of each recitation is different.

Hunter summarises the results of his researches as showing that lengthy verbatim recall occurs only in cultures where text exists and is used, and that it only occurs on a large scale in settings where a high value is placed upon text as a subject matter in its own right (e.g. among students of religious texts or works of literature). The encroachment of literacy into a previously non-literate society changes people's attitudes to language. One text can now be compared in detail with another across wide intervals of space and time. One version can be deemed to be true and correct, the other corrupt and distorted. Before the invention of writing that was not possible. With the advent of literacy, the precise wording of a religious or literary passage becomes a thing of importance that is not to be tampered with.

Learning Text Verbatim

If you *must* commit what you read to memory and learn it off by heart, then psychology can provide you with some tips on how to do it that are derived from the study of human memory in general. It will help to break the material down into smaller chunks. Intons-Peterson and Smyth (1987) gave two passages of text to subjects with instructions to learn them off by heart. Half the subjects had considerable experience of amateur dramatics and were used to memorising text; the other half had no special experience or training. The expert memorisers proved more efficient at breaking the passages down into suitable chunks for rehearsal and memorisation. They then used the initial words of each chunk as prompts for recalling the rest. Recall was excellent 2 days after learning for all except one subject, whose poor verbatim recall was attributed to a strategy of focusing on the meaning of the passage and attempting to recall its gist!

Material being learned by heart needs to be rehearsed over and over again. If the task is to learn the factual content of something, then the best form of rehearsal is "elaborative" rehearsal, in which the material is worked over, reflected upon and woven into pre-existing schema knowledge (Craik & Tulving, 1975). But elaborative rehearsal is of less value if verbatim recall is required. Here rote rehearsal is the only real option. The effectiveness of rehearsal and learning appears to be greatest if the same number of repetitions are spaced out over several sessions than if they are massed within a single session. Neisser summed this up nicely in a piece of doggerel which Baddeley (1990) repeats from Bjork (1988, p. 399):

You can get a good deal from rehearsal,
If it just has the proper dispersal.
But you would be an ass
To do it en masse:
Your remembering would turn out much worsal.

Baddeley also credits Neisser with formulating the "law" that if X appears interesting, it has not yet been studied. Hopefully that law permits the occasional exception.

FURTHER READING

Baddeley, A.D. (1990). *Human memory: Theory and practice.* Hove, UK: Lawrence Erlbaum Associates Ltd.

Eysenck, M.W. & Keane, M.T. (1990). *Cognitive psychology: A student's handbook* (2nd ed.). Hove, UK: Lawrence Erlbaum Associates Ltd.

Rayner, K. & Pollatsek, A. (1989). *The psychology of reading*. Englewood Cliffs, NJ: Prentice-Hall.
Smyth, M.M., Morris, P.E., Levy, P., & Ellis, A.W. (1987). *Cognition in action*. Hove, UK: Lawrence Erlbaum Associates Ltd.

CHAPTER SIX

Writing and Spelling

Thus far in the book we have concentrated on reading—on the processes involved in converting print to meaning and sound. In this chapter, we shall look at the reverse processes which allow the writer to express herself in writing. As compared with the amount of research devoted to the study of reading, the process of writing has been relatively neglected by psychologists. This may reflect the fact that almost everyone uses their reading skill much more than their writing skill; indeed, many adults never write anything more than the occasional note (if that). Most of the research that has been done on writing has focused on spelling; that is, on how we are able to remember and produce the string of letters that is accepted as the correct spelling of a particular word. Work on acquired disorders of writing has also tended to concentrate upon disorders of spelling. But generating the appropriate spellings of words comes relatively late in the writing process. If you are writing a letter or an essay, much of your mental energy is expended on deciding what you want to say, what order to make various points in, how to express yourself to maximum effect, and so on. It is with the planning of writing that we shall begin this chapter.

PLANNING TO WRITE

Compare the transcript of a casual conversation with a passage of text from a book and you will notice many differences. Typical speech has a simple grammatical structure and may lack clear sentence boundaries, is repetitive but rather inexplicit, is informal, and contains many pauses, ums, ers and false starts. In contrast, typical writing has a more complex grammatical structure, clear sentence boundaries, is explicit, formal and non-repetitive. Faced with such differences, one might be tempted to say that speech and writing use two quite different grammars, but it is probably more accurate to say that there is a continuum between the styles of spoken and written language rather than a dichotomy (Leech, Deuchar, & Hoogenraad, 1982). Thus, the language used in a personal letter between close friends may be more "speech-like" than the speech of a lecture or job interview. Writing tends more toward the formal end of the spectrum than speech, but the two overlap considerably.

Learning to write involves mastering the style of formal, written English. Someone who has been exposed to written English style through reading or listening may find it easier to produce their own writing than someone whose experience has been largely restricted to casual speech. Many people never feel comfortable expressing themselves in writing, and everyone experiences difficulties at first. Daiute (1981) examined the errors made by college students in their writing. Some errors involved marking as a sentence something which is only a sentence fragment (e.g. *Because the type of training the child gets is nothing compared to playing.*); others involved omissions of necessary words (e.g. *Mechanical devices have a tendency to lose students' attention.*). Of interest is the fact that, on average, the students were 11 words into a sentence before a lapse occurred. That is, they were trying to extend themselves beyond the lengths of the sentences of casual speech into the realms of formal English when their command of the complexities of that style momentarily failed them.

Hayes and Flower (1980; 1986) have produced one of the few theoretical accounts of the psychological processes involved in generating text. They note that many texts on "how to write" divide the process up into three broad stages—*pre-write*, *write* and *rewrite*. Pre-write encompasses all the reading around, evaluating and thinking which must be done before writing can begin. Hayes and Flower suggest that introducing writers to the notion of a pre-write phase can help remove some of the guilt often associated with "mulling over" or just gazing into space. Gould (1980) videotaped people writing letters and tried to estimate the amount of time spent planning, editing, rewriting, and so on. They suggest that roughly two-thirds of the total writing time is devoted to planning (i.e. to pre-write) and only one-third to writing and revising.

To write is to think. The act of trying to express oneself in writing can help to clarify the thoughts themselves and may throw up new ideas. This is Wason's (1980) view, developed after a study of academic writers. For instance, he quotes a historian who observed that, "One of the cheering things about writing is that it often clears my mind and stimulates ideas and directions of arguments which I had not thought of." Another writer comments in similar vein that, "Writing for me is an experience of knowing what to say. I can make endless schemes of how the piece should run but it never comes out according to plan. Until I have written a paragraph, I do not even know whether what I am saying is true. Once it is down in black and white I frequently see that it is not and then I have to ask myself why it is not" (Wason, 1980, p. 133).

The model of writing proposed by Hayes and Flower (1980; 1986) contains the separate elements pre-write, write and rewrite, but they are thought of as being in continuous interaction rather than being a linear sequence of stages. Within the space of a few seconds, a writer may be planning what to write next, writing the current sentence and then evaluating it to see if it does the job required of it. In Hayes and Flower's model, the initial planning of writing is influenced by the task environment (such things as the topic to be written about and the intended audience) and by the writer's long-term memory, which includes his or her knowledge of the topic, knowledge of the audience, and stored formulae or general plans for essay writing. Given this input, one must set about planning the content of the essay, bearing in mind certain constraints and goals such as the requirements to make the text comprehensible, memorable, persuasive or entertaining (see Collins & Gentner, 1980). Clearly these constraints will influence different writing assignments to different degrees. A thriller writer must be entertaining and comprehensible but need not be especially memorable, while an office memo need only aim at comprehensibility. In planning one must then organise the list of topics or ideas one wishes to mention into a logical order.

According to Hayes and Flower, planning involves non-linguistic, conceptual representations which could, for example, include extensive use of visual imagery. The necessity for ideas and concepts to be originally represented in an abstract "language of thought" can be appreciated if one reflects that many people can express the same ideas equally well in two or three different spoken languages, or that a series of instructions can often be conveyed as well, if not better, in a flow chart or series of pictures as in a series of sentences. Each "idea" or "topic" must then be broken down into a sequence of propositions which will be expressed in individual sentences or clauses. One then starts to write. Some writers formulate a very detailed plan before they start to write; others have only the sketchiest of outlines in their heads and let the topics organise themselves as they write. Some writers continuously monitor and edit their prose for spelling, grammaticality, accuracy of meaning and comprehensibility; others prefer to "get it all down" with minimal editing, then set about improving the product when they prepare a subsequent draft.

While practice at writing may improve and hone the skills we have just discussed, there is nothing to suggest that they are in any way unique to the production of written language. These descriptions of planning, translating, executing and monitoring must also characterise a storyteller in an oral culture, a best man preparing a wedding speech, a dissatisfied customer preparing what to say to the shop manager tomorrow, a child preparing his or her "class news", or an executive dictating a memo. Gould (1978) found that people who are good at writing are also typically good at speaking and dictating. Poor writers may be people whose ideas are never clearly formulated in the first instance or people who have great difficulty finding the right words to communicate their ideas. But formulating ideas and finding the right words are requirements of clear speech as much as clear writing, and difficulties with either impair both modes of language production.

SPELLING FAMILIAR WORDS

Speech and writing may share common processes as far as initial planning and sentence construction are concerned, but there must come a point where the two streams diverge, with speech leading to the articulation of phonemes and writing to the production of letters. Rightly or wrongly, society places as much emphasis on the ability to produce the correct sequences of letters as on the various other components of the writing skill. A job application may be beautifully composed in exquisite language, but if it is full of spelling errors it is unlikely to succeed.

The spelling errors of writers who have begun to master the rudiments of English spelling are often errors which sound like the word but are not the spellings accepted by convention as correct (e.g. SKOOL for SCHOOL, SIKOLOGY for PSYCHOLOGY). We noted in Chapter 1 that in the days before the invention of printing and dictionaries, such "errors" would have been acceptable because they communicate the sound of words adequately. However, English speakers now inhabit a world where each word has an accepted, correct spelling which would often be impossible to predict from the way the word is now pronounced. This is true even of very common words, giving us SHOULD not SHUD, ONE not WUN, BECAUSE not BIKOSS, WOMEN not WIMIN, and so on *ad infinitum*.

The vagaries of English spellings are such that the speller of English has no option but to memorise the conventional spellings of all familiar words. Cognitive models of spelling postulate a lexical store dedicated to retaining the spellings of familiar words (e.g. Ellis, 1982; Margolin, 1984; Morton, 1980). This store plays a role in writing analogous to the role that the speech output lexicon plays in speaking. We shall refer to it as the *graphemic output lexicon*.[1] Figure 6.1 shows how the graphemic output lexicon is related to the other components of one's language system.

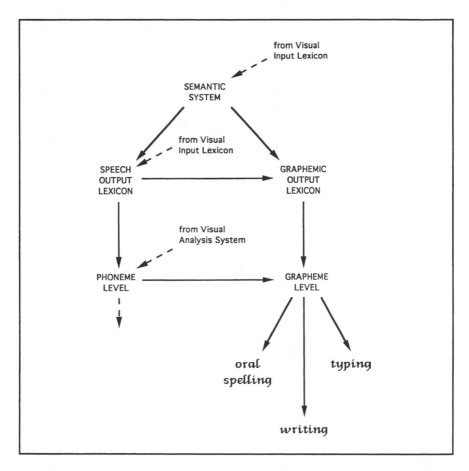

FIG. 6.1. Simple functional model of some of the cognitive processes involved in spelling single words.

The semantic system, speech output lexicon and phoneme level are components that should be familiar from Chapters 3 and 4. The graphemic output lexicon contains all those words whose spellings have been committed to memory. The reader will note that it receives two inputs—one from the semantic system and one from the speech output lexicon. This reflects the belief among cognitive psychologists and neuropsychologists that the spelling of a familiar word is retrieved in response to a dual specification of its meaning and sound-form. One line of evidence for this comes from errors made by skilled writers known as slips of the pen. A spelling error occurs when a writer does not know the correct spelling of a word, whereas in a slip of the pen the writer knows how the word should be written, but a momentary lapse results in something different being written.

Slips of the pen come in several different forms depending on whether the lapse involves whole words or individual letters, and whether it involves the simple subsitution or the movement of an intended element (Hotopf, 1980). The slips that have been used to make claims about inputs to the graphemic output lexicon involve the substitution of the intended word by another. Sometimes these are homophone errors where a writer writes, for example, THERE instead of THEIR or PIECE instead of PEACE. Sometimes they involve the production of a word that is similar but not identical to the intended word, such as writing SURGE for SEARCH or COULD for GOOD. Note that in all of these examples the writer knew full well how the intended word should be spelled. Note also that what is produced is another familiar word, not a guess at the spelling. Thus, a slip might involve writing THERE instead of THEIR, but never THAIR, and PIECE instead of PEACE, but never PEECE. That is, the error word is retrieved by mistake from the graphemic output lexicon in response to a specification of the sound-form of the intended word, a procedure represented in Fig. 6.1 by the input to the graphemic output lexicon from the speech output lexicon.

But although homophone and similar-sound slips occur, writers produce the correct versions of intended words most of the time. If the phonological form of an intended word was all that was available to guide its selection from the graphemic output lexicon, then writers would never be able to make a reliable selection between homophones. Morton (1980) suggested that the fact that homophones are usually spelled correctly could be explained if an additional input from the semantic system[2] was used to guide word choice. The function of the connection in Fig. 6.1 between the semantic system and the graphemic output lexicon is to provide such additional input. Thus, PIECE and PEACE have the same phonological forms, but their very different meanings should ensure that confusions between them are rare. Slips of the pen occasionally involve the substitution of an intended word by a different word that is similar in meaning rather than in sound (e.g. writing LAST WEEK for NEXT WEEK or SPEAKING for READING). The semantic system to graphemic output lexicon connection can also be held responsible for such errors.

The Grapheme Level

When considering speech production and reading aloud we introduced the concept of the phonemic level as a short-term store capable of holding a word's phonemic representation in the interval between being retrieved from the speech output lexicon and being articulated. Writing is slower than speaking, and there is need of an equivalent short-term store capable of holding a word's spelling between retrieval and execution, and capable of retaining the latter portion of a word while the earlier portion is being written. That is the primary function of the *grapheme level*[3] in Fig. 6.1.

The reader might be wondering why this new element in the model has been termed the *grapheme* level rather than the *letter* level. Is this just another case of psychologists using an obscure word where there is a perfectly adequate and more familiar alternative? Well, hopefully not entirely. The problem arises if one asks whether F and f are the same letter or two different letters? If they are two different letters, what term should be used to differentiate between them? Cognitive models of spelling and writing assume that a word's spelling is retrieved from the graphemic output lexicon in the same form whether the word is to be written in upper-case (CAPITAL) or lower-case (small) letters or, for that matter, whether it is to be written, typed or spelled aloud. The term "grapheme" has been chosen to denote the relatively abstract representation of a letter's identity which is retrieved from the graphemic output lexicon and held at the grapheme level and which is capable of being externalised in a variety of different ways.

SPELLING UNFAMILIAR WORDS

For a writer of English there seems no alternative to lexical storage and retrieval of the spellings of familiar words. It remains the case, however, that all skilled writers have the ability to devise plausible (if incorrect) spellings of unfamiliar words, and to create spellings in response to spoken nonwords. Patterson (1982) calls this procedure "assembled spelling". It involves breaking the unfamiliar word or nonword down into its component phonemes and converting those phonemes into appropriate graphemes. It is analogous to the procedure that allows a skilled reader to read aloud an unfamiliar word or nonword, but operates in the reverse direction—from phonemes to graphemes rather than from graphemes to phonemes—and is represented in Fig. 6.1 by the connection between the phoneme level and the grapheme level.

Spellings that are assembled using this sublexical procedure will have a chance of being correct if the word being attempted has a regular spelling, but if the word is irregular, the sublexical procedure will regularise it and produce what is sometimes referred to as a "phonic" or "phonetic" misspelling (for example, misspelling SCHOOL as SKOOL, WOMEN as WIMIN or YACHT as YOTT). Such errors are common in children's writing and are also seen in the writing of some patients with writing disorders. In both cases, they denote the use of the assembled spelling procedure for words that can only be spelled correctly by retrieval from the graphemic output lexicon.

In Chapter 3, we debated the question of how separate the whole-word and sublexical "routes" for reading aloud are. An experiment by Kay and Marcel (1981) was cited as evidence for some degree of interaction between those two procedures. To recap, Kay and Marcel (1981) showed that one can influence how normal subjects will pronounce a nonword like COTH by preceding it with either MOTH or BOTH. Campbell (1983) adapted this task to examine whether the spellings invented for dictated nonwords could be biased in a similar manner. Skilled writers were asked to spell nonwords which were preceded by real words. Campbell was able to show that a nonword like "prein" would tend to be spelled as PRAIN by subjects who had recently spelled the word BRAIN, but as PRANE by subjects who had recently spelled CRANE. This implies a degree of interaction between the lexical procedure involving the retrieval of spellings from the graphemic output lexicon and the sublexical procedure involving connections between the phoneme level and the grapheme level.

Although some of the spelling errors made by apprentice writers seem to be purely a result of assembly from phonology, others are not. Baron, Treiman, Wilf, and Kellman (1980) noted errors such as COLORNEL and COLNEL for colonel, RHYTHEM and RHYTHUM for rhythm, PNEWMONIA and PNEMONIA for pneumonia being made by university students. These writers knew that colonel has a silent L in it somewhere, that rhythm contains a silent H and a Y where an I might be expected, and that pneumonia begins with a silent P. That is, they possessed partial information about the spellings of these words, which they presumably combined with their knowledge of how to assemble spellings from sound to come up with a candidate spelling.

CENTRAL ACQUIRED DYSGRAPHIAS

In Chapter 4, we surveyed some of the ways in which injury to the brains of previously skilled readers can impair the reading process, giving rise to a range of acquired dysgraphias. The approach taken then was to try to explain each form of acquired dyslexia in terms of damage to one or more of the components of the normal reading system (though in the case of deep dyslexia we considered the possibility that it may reflect the functioning of a secondary, right hemisphere reading system operating in the virtual absence of the normal, left hemisphere system). Brain injury can also impair writing ability in people who were once competent spellers and writers, giving rise to a variety of forms of "acquired dysgraphia". Once again, the preferred mode of explanation will be in terms of damage to one or more of the components of the normal system—in this case, the writing system. Because almost all the work done on acquired dysgraphia has focused on the spelling of single words and their production in handwriting, we shall concentrate on disorders of those processes and not discuss possible disorders affecting higher-level planning processes.

Surface Dysgraphia

The condition known as "surface dyslexia", discussed in Chapter 4, is one in which patients seem no longer able to recognise and read many once-familiar words as whole units. Instead, they break them up and sound them out as if they were unfamiliar. The result is a particular difficulty with words that have irregular spellings and a tendency to regularise them. An analogous condition has been identified in writing and termed "surface dysgraphia". As with surface dyslexia, it is usually caused by damage to the left hemisphere of the brain (which in the majority of people is the hemisphere primarily responsible for language).

Hatfield and Patterson (1983) described a patient T.P. who seemed to have "forgotten" the conventional spellings of once-familiar words but remained good at devising plausible spellings from the sound-forms of words. The implication is that she has suffered damage affecting use of the graphemic output lexicon but retained some use of connections between the phoneme level and the grapheme level. Because the spellings of regular words are, by definition, the spellings you would expect on the basis of simple phoneme–grapheme (letter–sound) correspondences, T.P. was more successful at generating correct spellings to regular than irregular words. Her errors were predominantly regularisations, for example "nephew" spelled as NEFFUE, "biscuit" as BISKET and "subtle" as SUTTEL.

T.P. managed to spell some irregular words correctly on occasion, indicating that use of the graphemic output lexicon, though impaired, was not completely abolished. Sometimes she made homophone errors even when the word was dictated in a disambiguating sentence context (e.g. misspelling "sale" as SAIL, "write" as RIGHT and "sum" as SOME). This suggests that when she succeeded in retrieving the spelling of a word from the graphemic output lexicon, it was predominantly in response to a phonological input rather than a semantic input (i.e. she used the speech output lexicon to graphemic output lexicon connection rather than the connection from the semantic system).

When T.P. misspelled an irregular word, her errors sometimes demonstrated that she had partial information about the word's correct spelling. For example, she once misspelled "yacht" as YHAGT, demonstrating considerable knowledge of the eccentricities of that word's spelling. Other examples of this phenomenon include T.P. misspelling "borough" as PUROUGH and "sword" as SWARD. These errors are very like the student spelling errors we earlier attributed to "partial lexical knowledge", but whereas the student writers had never fully memorised the spellings of the words they erred on, it was the damage T.P. had incurred to her graphemic output lexicon that sometimes prevented her from fully recalling the spelling of a word she once knew.

In summary, T.P. could sometimes retrieve all of the spelling of a word from her graphemic output lexicon (evidenced by the fact that she could sometimes spell irregular words correctly). Sometimes she could recall something of a word's spelling but not enough to spell it correctly. Often, though, she could retrieve nothing from the graphemic output lexicon and was forced to attempt to assemble a spelling using her preserved capacity to map phonemes onto graphemes. Accounts of other patients with surface dysgraphia can be found in Ellis and Young (1988) and McCarthy and Warrington (1990).

Phonological Dysgraphia

Phonological dyslexia was discussed in Chapter 4 as a condition in which patients show a relatively well-preserved ability to read familiar words aloud, but are very poor at reading unfamiliar words or invented nonwords. An analogous condition, "phonological dysgraphia", can affect writing. Shallice (1981) reported the case of a patient, P.R., who spelled over 90% of a set of familiar words correctly but managed only two of ten simple four-letter nonwords like SPID and none of ten six-letter nonwords like FELUTE. When he managed to spell a nonword correctly, it appears to have involved the mediation of a real word (just as one might spell LEV correctly by stopping after the first three letters of LEVEL). Once again, Ellis and Young (1988) and McCarthy and Warrington (1990) provide further examples of this condition.

The experiments of Campbell (1983) and the analysis of the errors of both skilled writers and the surface dysgraphic patient T.P. all point to an interaction between the lexical procedure for whole-word spelling involving the graphemic output lexicon and the sublexical procedure for spelling unfamiliar words and nonwords that involves connections between the phoneme level and the grapheme level. Nevertheless, the contrast between surface dysgraphia (in which the whole-word procedure is impaired and the sublexical procedure is intact) and phonological dysgraphia (in which the reverse pattern is seen) suggests that these spelling procedures are to some degree distinct and separable. Their separation into phonological and surface dysgraphia provides what cognitive neuropsychologists call a double dissociation between the whole-word and sublexical spelling procedures. Such dissociations may be taken as evidence that there are cognitive processes involved in whole-word spelling that are not necessary for assembled, sublexical spelling, and vice-versa (see Shallice, 1988).

Deep Dysgraphia

In deep dyslexia, patients make semantic errors in reading aloud, read concrete words more successfully than abstract words and are virtually unable to read nonwords. The analogous condition has been reported for writing. Patients with "deep dysgraphia" make semantic errors when attempting to write words to dictation or to a write the names of objects. They are more successful at spelling concrete than abstract words and are virtually unable to write nonwords. Sometimes these patients are also deep dyslexic, in which case the semantic errors and the effect of concreteness would be ascribed to damage to the semantic system itself (e.g. patient G.R. of Newcombe & Marshall, 1980).

It is possible, however, to be deep dysgraphic without being deep dyslexic. Bub and Kertesz (1982) reported the case of a 21-year-old woman, J.C., who suffered a stroke which left her with halting, "telegraphic" speech and poor writing, but good comprehension of both spoken and written words. She made many semantic errors when writing words to dictation (e.g. "chair" written as TABLE, "time" as CLOCK, "yacht" as BOAT and "give" as TAKE) and was better at spelling concrete words than abstract words. Though she could repeat nonwords aloud, she was very poor at writing them, managing only 5/20 four-letter and 0/17 eight-letter nonwords. J.C.'s errors in this task sometimes took the form of writing a real word similar in sound to the dictated nonword (e.g. for "wabe" she wrote WADE, and for "besh" she wrote BASH). Such errors would seem to imply a similar strategy for spelling nonwords to that shown by Shallice's (1981) patient P.R. J.C. could even make semantic errors based on this strategy. For instance, when asked to spell "blom" she wrote FLOWER (presumably via "bloom"), and when asked to spell "lobinger" she wrote OYSTER (presumably via "lobster").

Bub and Kertesz report that J.C. appeared unaware that she was producing a semantic error as she wrote, but detected the error immediately after producing it. This and her intact reading comprehension suggest that J.C.'s semantic system was not damaged. The semantic errors must have arisen in transmission of activation from the semantic system to the graphemic output lexicon. If that connection was faulty, entries in the graphemic output lexicon for words similar in meaning to the intended word might sometimes have been activated (as perhaps in the semantic errors which occur in the slips of the pen of normal writers) and activation may have been more successfully communicated for the detailed meanings of concrete words than for the diffuse meanings of abstract words. Neuropsychological symptoms can arise as a consequence of damage to the connections between cognitive modules as well as through damage to the modules themselves.

The inability to write nonwords, implying loss of the connections between the phoneme level and grapheme level, may be a necessary condition for the occurrence of frequent semantic errors in writing. The knowledge that the initial phoneme of "chair" is usually written as CH, and is certainly never T, would otherwise prevent a patient from responding to "chair" with TABLE. Phonological dysgraphia, in which a similar loss of nonword spelling is seen without accompanying semantic errors, shows that more than just a loss of the sublexical spelling procedure is needed for semantic errors to occur, the extra deficit found in deep dysgraphic being either damage to the semantic system itself or damage to certain of its outputs.

PERIPHERAL WRITING PROCESSES AND PERIPHERAL DYSGRAPHIAS

We have mentioned that according to current models of the writing process, the contents of the grapheme level are capable of being outputted as handwriting, typing or spelling aloud (sometimes called oral spelling). Because such different end-products can be generated from the same representations, those representations (the graphemes) are argued to be relatively abstract in nature. We shall only concern ourselves here with conversion of graphemes into handwriting.

Current theories propose that two or three stages of planning intervene between the grapheme level and the movements of the arm, wrist and hand that produce handwriting on the page (Ellis, 1982; 1988; Van Galen, 1991). The first step involves selecting the particular letter shapes that are to be used. Is it to be A or a, B or b, H or h? The different forms that the same grapheme can take are sometimes referred to, following linguistic terminology, as *allographs*. H and h are two different allographs of the grapheme /h/. Which one is appropriate will depend on the context—Is this the first letter of a sentence or of a proper noun (e.g. Henry or Huddersfield)? Is the word being written in capital letters on a blackboard for clarity or in lower-case letters in a notebook?

After the allograph has been selected, the writer must then generate the sequence of movements that will result in the letters being written correctly. That movement sequence is sometimes called the "graphic motor pattern". It will specify the force and direction of the strokes needed to create the required size as well as shape of letters. All that is required to complete the writing process is for the graphic motor pattern to be implemented as a sequence of instructions by the necessary groups of muscles.

Problems with the different stages involved in converting graphemes into handwriting give rise to a whole additional set of acquired dysgraphias. Because these disorders affect the physical production of writing more than central knowledge of spellings or phoneme–grapheme correspondences, they are known collectively as "peripheral dysgraphias" (in contrast to central dysgraphias such as surface, phonological and deep dysgraphia). We shall consider only two here: accounts of others can be found in Ellis and Young (1988), McCarthy and Warrington (1990) and Margolin and Goodman-Schulman (1992).

Consider first what the effects of damage to the grapheme level itself might be. On the basis of Fig. 6.1, one would predict that the patient would have problems affecting the production of letter sequences, whether those sequences were to be written or spelled aloud. The grapheme level is involved in producing the spellings of familiar words retrieved from the graphemic output lexicon and in producing the spelling of unfamiliar words or nonwords assembled using connections between the phoneme level and the grapheme level; hence damage to the grapheme level should affect the spellings of familiar words and nonwords in the same ways.

A patient whose symptoms fitted this predicted pattern well was reported by Miceli, Silveri, and Caramazza (1985; 1987). Their patient, F.V., made errors of the same sort whether he was asked to spell words or nonwords, and whether he was asked to write or to spell aloud. The errors involved a mixture of additions, deletions, substitutions and transpositions (movements) of letters. The letters he wrote were, however, well formed, indicating that there were no additional problems tied to the selection of allographs or the execution of graphic motor patterns.

A very different form of peripheral acquired dyslexia was shown by patient V.B. (Ellis, Young, & Flude, 1987). We encountered this lady in Chapter 4 as an example of a patient with "neglect dyslexia", a condition exemplified by misreadings affecting the initial letters of words (e.g. misreading PEACH as "beach" or JAUNT as "haunt"). V.B. manifested a different problem in writing, one which has since been shown to be dissociable from neglect dyslexia. When V.B. tried to write words, she made numerous errors involving the omission or repetition of letters or strokes. Some examples are shown in Fig. 6.2.

The important difference between V.B. and the previous patient F.V. is that whereas F.V.'s problems extended to spelling aloud as well as handwriting, V.B.'s oral spelling was excellent. Indeed, when permitted to spell aloud she could out-perform the psychologists who tested her! Only when she was required to write did the errors occur. This establishes that central spelling process (including retrieval from the graphemic output lexicon) and storage and outputting from the grapheme level were all intact. V.B.'s problems lay downstream of the grapheme level.

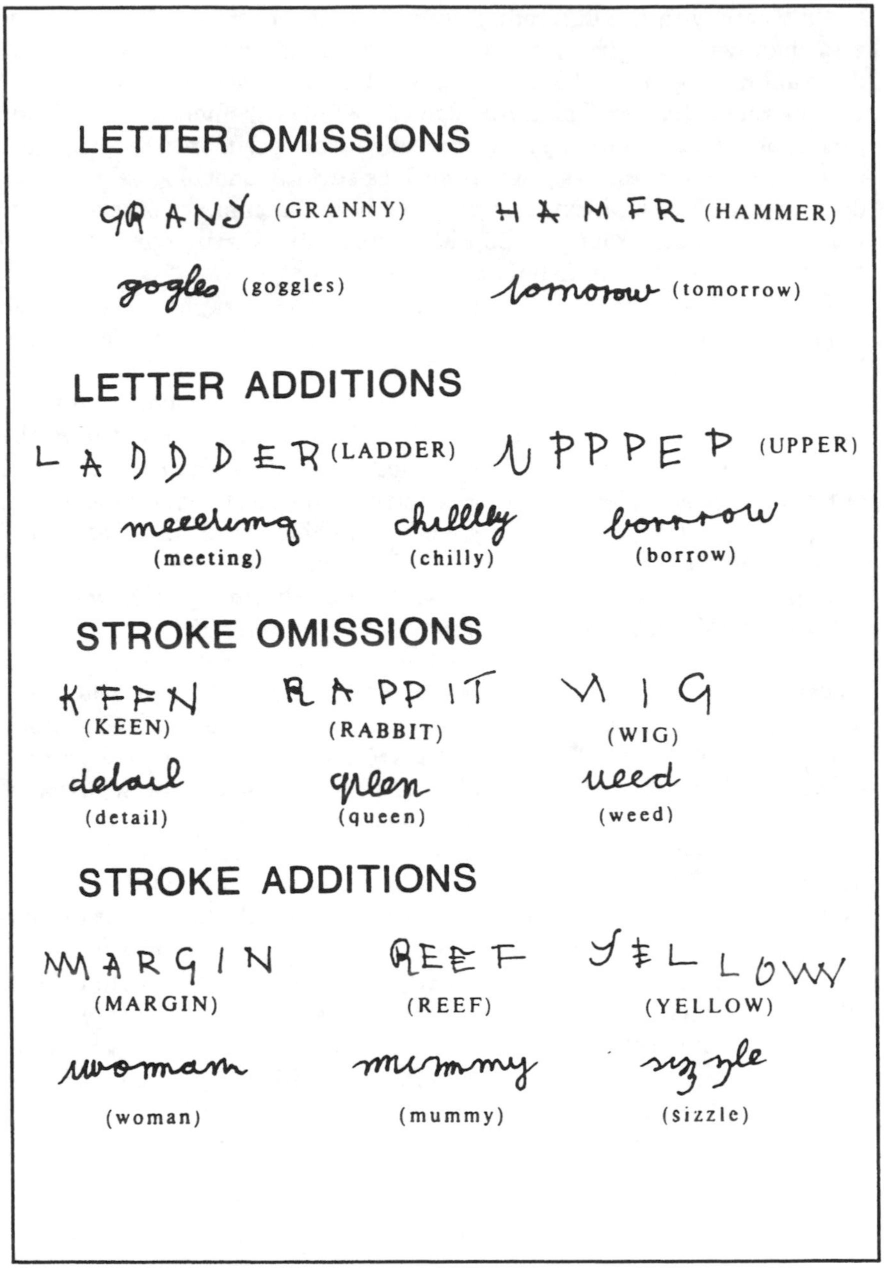

LETTER OMISSIONS

GR ANY (GRANNY)　　H Å M FR (HAMMER)

gogles (goggles)　　tomorow (tomorrow)

LETTER ADDITIONS

L A D D D E R (LADDER)　Λ P P P E P (UPPER)

meeelimg (meeting)　chillly (chilly)　borrrow (borrow)

STROKE OMISSIONS

K FFN (KEEN)　R A PP IT (RABBIT)　Ν I G (WIG)

detail (detail)　green (queen)　need (weed)

STROKE ADDITIONS

MM A R G I N (MARGIN)　REE F (REEF)　Y E L L OW (YELLOW)

wwomam (woman)　mummmy (mummy)　sizzle (sizzle)

FIG. 6.2. Examples of writing errors made by patient V.B. Reproduced with permission from A.W. Ellis, A.W. Young, and B.M. Flude (1987). "Afferent dysgraphia" in a patient and in normal subjects. *Cognitive Neuropsychology, 4,* 465–486.

NOTES

1. This lexicon was referred to in the first edition of *Reading, Writing and Dyslexia* as the "graphemic word production system".
2. The cognitive system of Morton's model.
3. Referred to in the first edition of *Reading, Writing and Dyslexia* as the "graphemic buffer".

FURTHER READING

Ellis, A.W. & Young, A.W. (1988). *Human cognitive neuropsychology.* Hove, UK: Lawrence Erlbaum Associates Ltd.

Frith, U. (Ed.). (1980). *Cognitive processes in spelling.* London: Academic Press.

Gregg, L.W. & Steinberg, E.R. (Eds.). (1980). *Cognitive processes in writing.* Hillsdale, NJ: Lawrence Erlbaum Associates Inc.

Margolin, D.I. & Goodman-Schulman, R. (1992). Oral and written spelling impairments. In D.I. Margolin (Ed.), *Cognitive neuropsychology in clinical practice.* New York: Oxford University Press.

McCarthy, R.A. & Warrington, E.K. (1990). *Cognitive neuropsychology: A clinical introduction.* San Diego, CA: Academic Press.

CHAPTER SEVEN

Learning to Read and Write

Modern societies expect virtually all children to learn to read. Before going on to consider how that skill is acquired, and might best be taught, it is worth pausing for a moment to reflect upon the fact that the current expectation of near-universal literacy is a very modern phenomenon. As Geschwind (1982, p. 22) observes: "... the overwhelming majority of humans who have ever lived have been illiterate, and even today I believe it is the case that a very large percentage, and perhaps the majority of the world's population have never had the opportunity to learn to read. Most of us come from families that four generations ago did not possess the ability to read." In most supposedly literate societies of the past, the ability to read and write was restricted to a small minority who might have been priests or professional scribes. The "secret" of literacy was often guarded closely by those who possessed it. It is only within the last 100 years or so that universal literacy has been a declared aim of many societies. We should keep that fact in mind when adjudicating on our success or failure in achieving that goal. But we should also keep in mind the fact that modern societies *assume* that their adult members can read. To be illiterate is to be at a profound disadvantage in the modern world.

PRE-READING

Children in different countries begin to learn to read at different ages. When Downing surveyed worldwide patterns in 1973, the age at which children received their first formal reading instruction varied from around

5 years in countries such as Great Britain, India and Uruguay, through 6 years in the United States, France and Japan, to 7 years in Denmark and Sweden. Between the 1930s and 1960s, it was not uncommon to encounter the claim being made that normal children needed to achieve a state of "reading readiness" before they could be successfully taught to read, and that this state was usually reached at around the age of 6½ years. Coltheart (1979) showed that the studies on which this claim was based simply could not bear the weight of the conclusions placed upon them, either because they were methodologically flawed or because they just did not find what they were commonly said to have found. Many children with a mental age of less than 6½ years make substantial progress in learning to read, though Coltheart (1979) reviews several studies showing that effort put into teaching children to read at a very early age has few, if any, long-term benefits, because the late starters soon catch up with the early achievers once they have begun to receive instruction.

In 1925, a group of 560 American teachers of first-grade (5- or 6-year-old) children were asked what, in their opinion, constituted "reading readiness". Their replies included appropriate comprehension, sufficient command of English, good speaking vocabulary, and wide and varied experiences (Holmes, 1928). These teachers knew what cognitive psychologists now assert, namely that reading draws on a wide range of psychological processes and skills, many of which are not specific to reading, and many of which begin their development well before children start to read. Successful word recognition depends on having a good vocabulary of spoken words, which includes knowing the meanings and uses of those words. Sentence and text comprehension depends on processes which are also used to understand spoken language, including general knowledge. The better a child's grasp of spoken language, and the better that child's knowledge of the world, the easier the business of learning to read and write should be, whenever that task is begun.

If the process of learning to read builds upon a foundation of other cognitive skills, then we should find that children who arrive at school with those skills well bedded in should make the easiest and best progress. That is the clear message of the research in this field. Much of that research has focused on what is termed "phonological awareness". This is the capacity to reflect upon and manipulate the sound structure of words and is assessed in tasks which range from deciding whether or not two words rhyme through deciding whether or not two words have the same initial sounds (phonemes) to removing phonemes from words and saying what is left (e.g. what is left if you remove the "s" from "stable"). All other things being equal, children who perform well on tests of phonological awareness before they begin any formal reading instruction learn to read faster than children with less well-developed phonological awareness (e.g. Helfgott, 1976;

Stanovich, Cunningham, & Cramer, 1984). Indeed, phonological awareness proves to be a better predictor of reading development than performance on intelligence tests (Wagner & Torgeson, 1987).

These studies look at the extent to which natural variation in phonological awareness before children learn to read predicts subsequent success. The implication is that training phonological awareness before children start school will help them learn to read. To test this prediction, Lundberg, Frost, and Peterson (1988) gave extensive phonological awareness training to a group of Danish pre-schoolers and showed that the reading and spelling of the trained children was superior to that of an untrained control group 2 years later. Hence, training phonological awareness in pre-school children helps reading development (though it must be admitted that the effects obtained in the Lundberg et al. study are quite small and one might query whether they justify the investment of time and energy).

We shall see shortly that phonological training that is allied to the teaching of reading a little later in a child's development can have much more substantial effects. It would be misleading, however, to imply that pre-school phonological ability is the only predictor of success in learning to read. A number of studies have found that a strong predictor of reading success is the fluency with which a pre-reader can identify (name) letters of the alphabet (e.g. Bond & Dykstra, 1967; Tunmer, Herriman, & Nesdale, 1988). This result may seem puzzling at first glance because letter names are of little obvious use in reading. Knowing that the the letters of HAT are named "aitch", "aye" and "tee" will not be of much help in identifying that word when it is encountered for the first time in print (though knowing the *sounds* those letters usually make will). It may be that being able to name letters fluently reflects the fact that a child has learned the appearance of letters and has learned to discriminate them one from another. Although the child cannot be said to be able to read yet, it has learned to distinguish b from d and p, m from w, n from u, and so on (Adams, 1990).

In terms of the model that guided our examination of skilled word recognition (see Fig. 3.1), the pre-reader with good phonological awareness has learned to reflect upon and manipulate the sound-forms of words that are stored at the phoneme level. For the skilled reader, those representations are active both in whole-word reading (via the visual input lexicon and speech output lexicon) and in the phonological reading procedures employed to identify words that are familiar through speech but have not been seen before (procedures that exploit direct connections between the visual analysis system and the phoneme level). It seems reasonable, therefore, that voluntary control and manipulation of the contents of the phoneme level should aid the development of reading when the time comes for formal tuition to begin.

The pre-reader with good letter naming may go on to learn to read more easily not because that child has learned the names of letters but because he or she has a head start in the creation of a visual analysis system. Just as the phoneme level forms a common output route for all reading procedures, so the visual analysis system forms a common input, identifying shapes as letters and feeding into both whole-word and phonological reading processes. Thus, the child equipped with both phonological awareness and letter identification skills arrives at the school gates with some of the aspects of the reading process already in place, meaning that less has to be acquired.

BEGINNING READING

So what happens to our child after he or she passes through the school portals and into the classroom? Some accounts of reading development would have us believe that children learning to read pass through an identifiable series of distinct stages in the acquisition of the skill. Such accounts show the influence of the Swiss psychologist Jean Piaget, who argued that the development of children's fundamental understanding of the physical world requires them to progress through a series of discrete psychological stages taking them from the understanding of the newborn to the understanding of the adult. When psychologists and linguists describe how children learn to talk, they typically invoke a set of distinct stages. It is perhaps inevitable, therefore, that psychologists trying to explain reading development have also felt drawn towards stage models (e.g. Ehri, 1993; Frith, 1985; Marsh, Friedman, Welch, & Desberg, 1981). The models differ in their particulars, but share a number of common features which we shall emphasise here.

Words as Pictures

It is commonly proposed that in the very earliest stages of reading development, written words are identified purely on their visual appearance, almost as one might recognise an object or picture. Some of the characteristics of children at this stage have been described by Seymour and Elder (1986). They observed the reading development of the individual members of a class of 4- to 5-year-olds over the course of their first year in a Scottish school. The instruction they received emphasised the formation of a "sight vocabulary". There was no discussion at all of letter–sound correspondences in the first two terms. When the children were asked to read single words aloud, most of the children could read the specific words they had been taught, but only one of the 26 children in the class could read an appreciable number of unfamiliar words. He was the most successful reader in the class, and seemed to have worked out some letter–sound correspondences for himself. None of the other 25 children had managed this, however.

There were several other indicators that the children were identifying familiar words on a purely visual basis, making no use of letter–sound correspondences. The speed with which the children could name individual words was unaffected by the number of letters in each word, suggesting that they were recognising them as whole visual patterns. When children misread words, they tended to read them as other words from the vocabulary they had been taught. Their comments indicated that they were using simple visual features to identify the words. For example, one child misread smaller as "yellow" because of the double-l in the middle, commenting, "It's "yellow" because it has two sticks". Another child responded "black" to almost anything of approximately the right length that ended in k. Occasionally, the children would produce a word similar in meaning to the written word, for example misreading *boat* as "yacht" or *little* as "wee" (= small in Scots). It appears that in these instances, the printed word was recognised and activated a meaning in the child's mind, but that the wrong spoken word was then produced. Wells (1906, pp. 77–78) reports an intriguing case of a child who was taught to read entirely by the look-and-say method and who apparently made semantic errors such as misreading *corn* as "wheat", *locomotive* as "engine" and *dog* as "cat".

With no grasp of letter–sound correspondences, children at this stage cannot "sound out" unfamiliar words they encounter. All they can do is guess. If the unfamiliar word is encountered in a sentence or story, a child may guess at a likely word using the previous context as a guide. For example, if the word *rocket* is not yet part of a child's sight vocabulary, then that child might read *The boy went to the moon in a rocket* as "The boy went to the moon in a spaceship", using the context to make a plausible guess at the last word. Critchley and Critchley (1978) called these errors "narremic substitutions". They went on to draw a parallel between them and the semantic errors made by acquired deep dyslexics. This parallel is misguided, however, because of the different situations in which the errors occur. The child who reads *The boy went to the moon in a rocket* as "The boy went to the moon in a spaceship" does, in a sense, produce a semantic error by misreading *rocket* as "spaceship", but we could replace rocket by *cauliflower* in the above sentence and the child would just as readily assert that the boy travelled to the moon in a spaceship! It is easy to be misled by the semantic relationship between rocket and spaceship into thinking that the child has extracted some meaning from rocket, whereas what has probably happened is that the child has used the context to make a plausible guess.

The Addition of Phonics

The typical young child will not spend very long at the first stage. Soon he or she will either notice or be taught that the spellings of words bear some relationship to their sounds. In other words, the child will begin to learn something about "phonics". At first, this is limited to simple letter–sound correspondences. On encountering an unfamiliar word, the child will attempt to "sound it out", working through the word from left to right. Words like PIN and DAM may be read successfully because their letter–sound correspondences are simple, but PINE and DAME may be pronounced "pinneh" and "dammeh" because the child does not yet know how to apply more complex rules like the one which says that a final e can lengthen the preceding vowel. When more complex aspects of spelling–sound relationships are learnt, we cannot say for certain that the knowledge in question is actually embodied in the child's mind as abstract rules. Goswami (1986) showed that if 6- to 7-year-olds were taught to read a previously unfamiliar word like HARK, they were more likely to go on to read correctly another unfamiliar word with a similar spelling (e.g. LARK). This is reminiscent of Kay and Marcel's (1981) demonstration that recent experience with familiar words can influence how adults pronounce a nonword and suggests that whole-word and phonological reading procedures interact in children as they do in adults.

With the acquisition of a more complex understanding of spelling–sound relationships, the young reader effectively becomes a skilled reader. His or her vocabulary will continue to enlarge as new words are registered in the visual input lexicon and the speech output lexicon and as new meanings enter the semantic system. The operation of these and other component reading processes will increase in speed and efficiency, but essentially the system is an adult one. The fact that a word encountered for the first time in lower-case print will subsequently be recognised without difficulty when seen in capital letters shows that recognition is no longer pictorial but rather involves the intervention of a visual analysis system and visual input lexicon.

It will be some time before the visual input lexicon and the speech output lexicon develop to include all the words that form part of a skilled reader's vocabulary. Meanwhile, the apprentice reader will often encounter words that he or she has not seen before (though these will often be words that have been encountered in speech and whose meaning is known). The presence of some phonological reading capability should mean that the child can identify such words provided that they have reasonably regular spellings. Intelligent use of context should also help narrow down the range of possible options when an unfamiliar word is encountered in text. Once an unfamiliar word has been identified once or twice using a combination of phonics and context, it should become registered in the visual input lexicon and should be recognised as a familiar word thereafter. Hence, the child possessed of some phonic reading skill is a much more independent reader than the child who lacks phonics, and can build up a "sight vocabulary" with less need of external assistance.

Criticisms of Stage Models

The sort of stage account of reading development just described may characterise the reading development of many children, but is this sequence universal in the way that Piaget thought his stages of cognitive development to be universal? Reading, as we have noted before, is not a natural skill, but is an artificial skill that is culturally transmitted from one generation to the next (more like driving or knitting than walking or talking). Stage theories tend to assume that all children are alike and are taught in much the same way, but that may not be a reasonable assumption. In colonial America, the teaching of reading was highly phonic from the outset (Venezky, 1980). The teaching methods one would observe in a class of beginning American readers in the 1780s would be very different from those that Seymour and MacGregor (1984) observed in use with young Scottish children in the 1980s. The old American way began by teaching children the alphabet and the sound values of letters. Only when they had been mastered were whole words introduced. Under such circumstances, it would be most surprising if a "visual" stage without any application of phonics could be observed. The "stages" documented by both American and British psychologists in the 1980s may be very much a reflection of the styles of teaching reading in vogue at the time. Stuart and Coltheart (1988) argue on the basis of a longitudinal study of the early reading development of a group of children in London that not all children pass through the same sequence of stages, and that for some children the very earliest stage of word recognition includes some use of phonological knowledge of letter–sound correspondences.

Individual Differences in Children's Reading

By the age of, say, 7 or 8 years, the average child will have begun to establish a "sight vocabulary", i.e. will have begun to build up a visual input lexicon. Many words that adults know will not yet have been learned, but because the child has some understanding of letter–sound correspondences, he or she will be able to "sound out" these visually unfamiliar words. This process should generate the correct pronunciation if the word being attempted has a regular spelling, but if it is irregular in its spelling, the result will be a regularisation error. This characteristic pattern of young children's reading has been documented by Backman, Bruck, Hebert, and Seidenberg (1984) and Waters, Seidenberg, and Bruck (1984).

Not all children are alike, however, in the extent to which they use whole-word and phonological processes in reading. Baron and Strawson (1976) and Baron (1979) used tests of word and nonword reading to identify children whose reading relied heavily on whole-word recognition and contrasting children who relied heavily on letter–sound conversion. The former group were dubbed "Chinese" readers because reading of real Chinese is logographic and depends on whole-word processing. The latter group were dubbed "Phoenecian" readers after the Mediterranean people who perfected the alphabet. Readers of English who are of the "Chinese" type recognise words as visual wholes—they recognise irregular words as readily as regular words, but are poor at reading aloud nonwords. Because of their emphasis on sublexical letter–sound conversion, "Phoenecians" read regular words more accurately than irregular words and are good at reading nonwords. Treiman (1984) showed that whole-word "Chinese" readers tended also to be whole-word spellers whose difficulties in using letter–sound correspondences in reading were mirrored by difficulties using sound–letter correspondences in spelling unfamiliar words and non-words. Phonological ("Phoenecian") readers tended likewise to be phonological spellers.

Stuart and Masterson (1992) have shown how individual differences in children's reading patterns might relate to the levels of phonological awareness they showed as pre-readers. They examined the reading of a group of 10-year-olds who they had first assessed as 4-year-old pre-readers. The children with higher scores on phonological awareness tasks as 4-year-olds proved to be better readers at age 10. In addition to having higher reading ages, they showed larger regularity effects, were better at nonword reading, and made more phonological reading errors than children who had scored lower on phonological awareness tasks 6 years previously.

TEACHING READING

We have already noted that the methods used to teach reading vary from place to place and from time to time. Throughout the twentieth century, battles have raged among "experts" (though less, perhaps, among practising teachers) over how reading should best be taught. We shall begin by reviewing a few of the more commonly used methods and will then discuss some of their strengths and weaknesses. Fuller coverage of a wider range of methods, their rationales and the evidence for or against them can be found in Chall (1983) and Adams (1990).

"Whole-word" (or "look-and-say") methods encourage children to recognise words directly, as visual units. This may, for example, involve the use of "flash cards" with single words written on them which children learn to recognise. Objects around the classroom will have their names attached to them. Relations between component letters and phonemes of words are not made explicit. This method, which is sometimes also referred to as a "meaning-based approach", became the dominant approach in America in the 1930s and is still widespread there (Adams, 1990). The "language experience" approach is very similar, except that the children are taught reading and writing together. They are encouraged to think of things to write down, then practise reading the same words and sentences. The idea is that because children choose their own topics and use their own vocabulary, the material should be of interest to them, and the words and concepts should be familiar. The correspondences between written and spoken words are made explicit, but not the correspondences between letters and sounds.

"Phonics" approaches deliberately teach letter–sound correspondence to children who learn the pronunciations typically given to letters and letter groups. Reading aloud may be referred to as "decoding". Children are taught to break words down into their component letters and "sound them out". Stories the children are given to read will initially contain short words with simple, regular spellings that are relatively simple to sound out. Words incorporating more complex spelling–sound correspondences will be introduced later along with words which have irregular spellings.

The "linguistic method" is somewhat similar, but involves presenting stories to beginning readers in which particular letter–sound correspondences are repeated. Children are meant to deduce these correspondences for themselves as much as possible. Crowder (1982, p. 208) provides the following example of a typical "story":

Dad had a map
Pat had a bat
Tad had a tan cap
Nan had a tan hat.

One would like to think that a choice of one teaching method over another would be based on hard evidence showing that children taught by one approach learn to read better than children taught by a different method. Most of the time, alas, one would be wrong. Evidence has been around for a long time, but until recently it has been possible either to dispute the evidence or to ignore it completely. Under such circumstances, policy is determined by fashion and the zeal of enthusiasts for one approach. Literacy is the loser. More and better studies are now being reported, however, providing a firmer basis for the choice of teaching method.

It may also be that more attention is being given to evidence (as opposed to advocacy) because of widespread concern over reading standards. Research in America, for example, has shown that in the 1980s, 75% of the unemployed, 85% of juveniles appearing in court, 60% of prison inmates and 30% of semi-skilled and unskilled workers were "functionally illiterate"; that is, they fell short of the most basic level of literacy required to function adequately in a modern society—to read newspapers, notices, application forms, and so on (Orton Dyslexia Society, 1986). Adams (1990) produces a chilling catalogue of statistics of that sort.

So what data exist that might permit a rational choice of teaching methods? Basically, the evidence is of two sorts. First, researchers can try to take advantage of the fact that different schools may employ different methods. It may be possible to find a sample of schools where a whole-word approach predominates and to compare the progress of the children in those schools with that of children in schools which place more emphasis on phonics. Alternatively, the researcher may undertake an intervention study to examine the effect of giving different types of additional reading tuition above that which is provided in the home and classroom. Both methodologies have their strengths and weaknesses but, as we shall see, the conclusions which emerge from them are broadly similar.

Surveys of Different Teaching Methods in Normal Use

Surveying different teaching methods in normal use is fraught with difficulties. One might at first blush think that it would be a straightforward matter to compare the progress of children in classes or schools in which different teaching methods are employed. The problem is that two schools may differ in their approach to the teaching of reading, but they may also differ in 101 other respects such as the nature of their catchment areas, the degree of parental support and involvement, the amount of money available to spend on teaching materials, the commitment of the teachers to the methods they are supposed to be using, and so on. Different methods of teaching reading may also tend to go hand in hand with different ways of organising classrooms, phonics tending to be found in traditional "teacher-centred" classrooms and meaning-based, whole-word methods in more loosely organised "student-centred" class-rooms (Evans & Carr, 1985). Given enough different teachers and schools, and relevant data on all these factors, it may be possible to draw valid conclusions, but it is very difficult.

Despite the problems, many studies have been published comparing this method of teaching reading with that method. Most commonly, whole-word methods are contrasted with phonic methods, that being the dimension along which the controversies lie. In the 1960s, the US Office of Education co-ordinated a large-scale study looking not only at reading methods, but also at the notion of reading readiness and the impact of pupil, teacher, classroom, school and community characteristics on reading progress in the first year of schooling. The results, published by Bond and Dykstra (1967), indicated that children given explicit training in phonics out-performed children taught by whole-word methods at the end of the first year. That seemed to be especially true when phonics teaching was combined with experience of reading stories and other connected texts. There was no evidence that the superiority of one method over another varied with the ability level (or "readiness") of the child being taught. A more recent study by Evans and Carr (1985) again found a superiority for phonics over whole-word methods (or, in their terms, for "decoding-oriented" over "language-oriented" approaches). This superiority extended to measures of text comprehension: there is no evidence to support any claim that teaching phonics interferes with or detracts from a child's comprehension of things read (Perfetti, 1985).

Bond and Dykstra (1967) and Evans and Carr (1985) represent two of the better examples of this genre, but the enterprise is, as was noted, fraught with difficulty. An alternative, and arguably better, approach to comparing the efficacy of different teaching methods is to take matched groups of children from comparable backgrounds and then to examine the effectiveness of different types of controlled intervention on their reading development. It is to such studies that we now turn.

Intervention Studies

Intervention studies take children out of their normal classrooms for periods of time and give them various forms of extra tuition. The capabilities of the children are assessed at the beginning of the tuition and again at the end, with a view to seeing if the different forms of training have differential effects.

Bradley and Bryant (1983; 1985) assessed the phonological awareness of 403 four- and five-year-olds in the Oxford area. None of the children had any measurable ability to read or spell at the outset of the study. Phonological awareness was tested by giving the children three or four 3-letter words, all but one of which had the same initial, middle or final sound. The child's task was to say which word was the "odd man out". For example, if the experimenter said "lot, cot, hat, pot", then the child had to identify "hat" as the odd man out. In line with the findings of studies mentioned earlier, the performance of the pre-schoolers on this phonological awareness task was found to be a good predictor of their reading and spelling ability over 3 years later.

Bradley and Bryant then selected 65 of the children who had poor phonological awareness at the age of 6 and divided them into four groups. The four groups were given different forms of training spread over 2 years. The first group was given sound categorisation training, working on their appreciation of rhyme and alliteration using pictures and spoken words, but not written words. The second group received similar training, but this time plastic letters were introduced to teach the children in this group something of the relationship between letters and sounds. The remaining two groups were control groups of different types. One control group received training that was unrelated to phonological awareness (classifying words into semantic categories); the other received no training at all.

The study achieved some impressive results. When reading was assessed at the end of the intervention (by which time the children were 8 years old), the reading level of the group which had been taught sound categorisation plus letter–sound relationships was a full 14 months ahead of the reading level of the group which had received no training at all. The combination of phonological awareness training with training on letter–sound correspondences proved to be highly effective in enhancing reading development.

That finding is reinforced by an American study by Cunningham (1990). Here, one group of 5- to 6-year-old children received phonological awareness training without reference to letter–sound relationships, a second group received phonological awareness training where the value of such things as segmentation and blending to reading was made explicit, while the third (control) group listened to and discussed stories. Training was given in 15- to 20-min sessions, twice a week for 10 weeks. The two experimental groups improved equally on tests of phonological awareness, but as in the Bradley and Bryant study, the reading performance of the children given phonological awareness training that was explicitly related to the task of reading improved more than that of the children given pure phonological awareness training only.

We noted earlier that for many children, the earliest stage of reading development involves an almost pictorial identification of words as visual patterns. It is not obvious why improved awareness of phonology and letter–sound relationships should enhance reading at this stage, since the sound patterns of words seem not to be invoked in the act of recognition. Perhaps children with improved awareness spend less time at this first stage, start to use phonic strategies earlier, and hence learn to read faster. Alternatively, there may never be a stage for such children at which word recognition is purely pictorial; these children may utilise some degree of phonic decoding from the outset.

The Cumbria–York study (Hatcher, Hulme, & Ellis, in press) involved children who had already experienced at least 2 years of schooling. At the outset of this study, all the 6- and 7-year-olds in the third year of infant school across a wide area of England's Lake District were given a standard reading test. One hundred and eighty-eight children were identified as having reading quotients of less than 86 (where a reading quotient of 100 would represent average reading ability). These children form roughly the bottom 10% in terms of reading ability. Children with severe general learning difficulties were then excluded from the study, and the remaining children were divided into four groups of 32, matched on age, sex, intelligence and reading ability. Before the intervention began, a suite of tests was administered, looking at a variety of reading and cognitive abilities, including the reading of single words, the reading and comprehension of passages of text, spelling to dictation, phonological awareness and arithmetical skills.

The four groups were then assigned to different training conditions. One group was the control group. These children received their normal classroom teaching, but no additional tuition. The children in the remaining three groups each received 40 half-hour sessions of extra tuition spread over 20 weeks (an amount of extra tuition that was thought to be realistic in an educational context). Twenty-three teachers were involved in the intervention.

The children in the *phonology only* group practised a range of phonological tasks which used pictures and spoken words as materials and required spoken responses or, occasionally, pointing. No reading or writing was done during the training, which was geared purely towards improving the children's phonological awareness.

The children in the *reading plus phonology* group received an integrated package which combined phonological training with reading instruction that was adapted from a teaching package used with apparent success in New Zealand and elsewhere (Clay, 1985; 1987). The phonological tasks included things like rhyme detection, identifying the phonemes (sounds) at different positions in simple words and using counters to indicate the number of sounds in words. The sound structure of words was explicitly related to the spellings of the same words through phonic tasks which involved, for example, segmenting spoken words and then building them up with plastic letters, or changing letters in words and noting the effect on the sound of the word. Tasks with a more whole-word or language experience type of approach included cutting up stories into words and then recreating the story by matching the words back to a model, using the meaning of text just read to guess what a difficult word might be, reading well-known texts along with the teacher, and making a game out of reading quickly.

Finally, the training package for children in the *reading only* group was the same as that for those in the reading plus phonology group, except that all the phonological tasks were removed, along with those reading tasks that taught the relations between spellings and sounds. The training in this condition therefore concentrated on the whole-word and language experience types of training.

The battery of assessment tests was repeated at the end of the intervention. Bearing in mind that the children were all now at least 20 weeks older than when the battery was first given, and had received normal schooling during that period, we must expect all the groups to have progressed somewhat. In order to know whether any of the interventions had been effective, we need to establish that the improvement in one or other of the intervention groups was significantly greater than that shown by the control group.

Unsurprisingly, perhaps, the children in the phonology only group tended to show the greatest improvement on the phonological awareness tasks (sound deletion, blending, nonword segmentation and sound categorisation), followed by the reading plus phonology group. The improvement of the reading only group on the phonological awareness tasks was no greater than that of the controls. Thus, reading tuition which does not make the links between spellings and sound patterns explicit may make little difference to children's general phonological ability.

Accuracy of reading single words aloud improved more in the reading plus phonology group than in the control group. Neither the reading only group nor the phonology only group improved more than the controls on accuracy of single word reading. The same was true of accuracy of text reading, where the reading plus phonology group was the only group to show an improvement that was significantly greater than the improvement made by the control group over the 20 weeks of the intervention.

One might have thought that visual reading training would come into its own when comprehension of text was assessed by asking questions concerning the content of passages read. In fact, the reading only group did improve more than the controls on the comprehension scores, but even greater improvement was shown by the reading plus phonology group. Reading accuracy and reading comprehension are not competitors, but go hand in hand because successful comprehension of a passage of text depends on successful identification of its component words. If better phonic skills means better word identification, then it will mean better comprehension too.

The reading plus phonology group was the only intervention group to show an improvement in spelling ability greater than that of the controls, while none of the interventions caused improvements in arithmetical skills greater than those shown by the controls. This latter finding is important because it shows that involving the children in intervention procedures did not have any general facilitatory effects on classroom performance. The improvements obtained were specific to reading and spelling.

An intervention package may have short-term benefits, but do its effects last? If they do not, then one might not feel justified in implementing the package on any large scale. The children who took part in the Cumbria–York study were re-tested 9 months after the end of the intervention. Effects of the intervention could still be seen, even after such an interval. The group who had received the reading plus phonology training continued to outscore the other three groups on both reading accuracy and comprehension, though the scores of thereading only group and the phonology only group were now both indistinguishable from the scores of the controls. Only reading training with an integrated phonological component conveyed durable benefits.

Groups of children may improve to degrees that are statistically significant, but the amount of improvement may still be relatively small, and not enough to warrant the investment of resources required. One way to express the degree of improvement on standardised tests is as an improvement ratio. If a child's reading age improves by 8 months over a period of 8 months, then that child's improvement ratio would be 1.00 (i.e. the child would be progressing as expected). If the reading age advanced by only 4 months the ratio would be 0.5 (i.e. the child would be progressing only half as fast as expected), whereas if it advanced by 16 months the ratio would be 2.0 (i.e. the child would be progressing twice as fast as expected). Over the period of the intervention, the children in the control group of the Cumbria–York study showed improvement ratios of 1.16 on accuracy of text reading and 0.54 on comprehension. That is, their reading accuracy, though generally poor, was keeping pace with their age, but their reading comprehension was falling even further behind. By comparison, the children in the reading plus phonology training group showed improvement ratios of 1.91 on accuracy of text reading and 2.05 on comprehension. That is, their reading accuracy and comprehension both came on twice as fast as one would have expected them to. In fact, if we bear in mind that the improvement ratio of the control group on comprehension was 0.5, the reading comprehension of the reading plus phonology group could be said to have improved four times more than it would have done if the children in that group had received only their normal classroom teaching.

In summary, two 30-min sessions of extra tuition given to 6- and 7-year-old poor readers for 20 weeks produced substantial and lasting improvements in reading and spelling if the tuition involved teaching children the relationships between the sound structure of English words and their spellings. Comprehension of what was read improved, not just the capacity to read words aloud. Neither pure phonological awareness training unrelated to reading, nor visual, whole-word training achieved anything like the same results; indeed, such improvement as was made by children receiving those forms of tuition was often no greater than that of children receiving only ordinary classroom teaching. If we wish to base our educational recommendations on evidence rather than politics or fashion, then all the evidence to date strongly favours teaching methods that incorporate a clear, systematic phonic element.

One last point to note is that reading tuition can occur outside as well as inside school. Hewison (1988) reports the results of a study in which efforts were made to increase parental involvement in teaching children to read. In particular, the parents were encouraged to spend time every week reading along with their children and discussing what was read. Three years after completion of the project, the children whose parents had been involved were reading significantly better than children whose parents were not recruited to the study.

LEARNING TO WRITE

Just as there has been less research into skilled writing than skilled reading, so there has been less work done on how children learn to write than on how they learn to read. There is much involved in learning to read. Some children try to write from as early as 3 or 4 years of age. At this age they know the correct spellings of hardly any words, so make them up as they go along. Descriptions of such children and their spellings have been provided by Read (1971), Chomsky (1970) and Bissex (1980). These early invented spellings tend to be very sound-based; the children spell words as they say them, for example writing CHRIBLS for "troubles" and JRAGIN for "dragon". These may at first blush seem bizarre, but in casual speech the initial /t/ of "troubles" can come out more like "ch" than "t", and the initial /d/ of "dragon" can come out more like "j" than "d".

A phonic approach to spelling seems to come quite naturally to most children, and they will spell phonically at a stage when their reading is very visual, with little or no evidence of use of phonics. This was demonstrated neatly by Bryant and Bradley (1980), who gave some normal 6- and 7-year-olds a list of 30 words to read on one occasion and to write on another. They found that being able to read a word was no guarantee of being able to spell it, and vice versa. The four words most commonly read correctly but misspelled were school, light, train and egg. These are all visually rather distinctive words which cannot reliably be spelled by phonic (sublexical) means (compare SKULE, LITE, TRANE and EG). In contrast, the four words most commonly spelled correctly but read incorrectly were the visually non-descript words BUN, PAT, LEG and MAT, words whose spellings nevertheless have a fair chance of being successfully predicted from their sounds. Interestingly, many of the same 6- and 7-year-olds later succeeded in reading BUN, PAT, LEG and MAT correctly when those words were embedded in a list of nonwords which obliged the children to adopt a phonic reading strategy. Bryant and Bradley's children seem to have preferred to read visually, though they could switch to assembling pronunciations phonically when forced. They often failed, however, to make this switch spontaneously.

Most poor readers are also poor spellers, but there are quite a few people around who are poor spellers while being reasonably good readers. Frith (1978; 1980) assembled a group of teenage good readers/poor spellers. Careful investigation of their reading showed that although their reading ages were normal, their word recognition was very "visual" in nature; they were whole-word readers with poor phonological reading skills (evidenced by poor nonword reading). In contrast, their spelling was highly phonic. We could say that they were "Chinese" readers but "Phoenecian" spellers. This is the same pattern as Bradley and Bryant observed in their 6- to 7-year-old children, though Frith's subjects were several years older. In both cases, reading and writing show very different characteristics: reading is done on a whole-word basis with poor sublexical letter–sound conversion skills, whereas spelling is heavily dependent on sublexical conversion (this time sound-to-letter) with difficulties implied in the whole-word storage of spellings. This "crossover" pattern between reading and spelling implies some degree of independence between the processes involved in recognising written words and those involved in producing them. This has educational implications: teachers should not assume that because a child can read a word correctly, that child will also be able to spell the word. If reading and writing are based on at least partially separate sets of cognitive processes, they will need to be taught separately.

FURTHER READING

Adams, M.J. (1990). *Beginning to read: Thinking and learning about print*. Cambridge, MA: MIT Press.

Bryant, P. & Bradley, L. (1985). *Children's reading problems*. Oxford: Basil Blackwell.

Chall, J.S. (1983). *Learning to read: The great debate* (2nd ed.). New York: McGraw-Hill.

Goswami, U. & Bryant, P. (1990). *Phonological skills and learning to read*. Hove: Lawrence Erlbaum Associates Ltd.

Oakhill, J. & Garnham, A. (1988). *Becoming a skilled reader*. Oxford: Basil Blackwell.

CHAPTER EIGHT

Developmental Disorders of Reading and Writing

We noted in the previous chapter that it is only in the last 100 years or so that the goal of universal literacy has arisen in Western societies. Hence it is not surprising to discover that it was about 100 years ago that the first accounts appeared of children who, despite normal or above-normal intelligence, apparently normal hearing and eyesight, and an adequate home background, had inordinate difficulty learning to read and write. Credit for the first systematic reports of unexpected reading difficulties in children is usually shared between two British doctors, James Kerr and Pringle Morgan, both of whom presented their ideas publicly in 1896. Neither seems to have taken their observations further, but the idea was taken up by a Scottish ophthalmologist, James Hinshelwood, whose work is summarised in *Congenital Word-blindness* (1917).

In America, the concept of "developmental dyslexia" was promoted by Samuel T. Orton, whose *Reading, Writing and Speech Problems in Children*, published in 1937, was highly influential. It was Orton who argued that dyslexia is more common in individuals who are neither firmly right-handed nor firmly left-handed. Although this claim is well known, widely believed and oft-repeated, it has proved remarkably difficult to obtain unequivocal evidence to support it (Bishop, 1990).

Central to the concept of developmental dyslexia is the idea of *unexpected* reading problems; that is, the idea that some children may experience difficulties with the acquisition of reading and writing that cannot be attributed to poor hearing or vision, low intelligence or inadequate educational opportunities. This concept is embodied in the various definitions of dyslexia at large in medical and educational circles. For example, the definition of dyslexia proferred by the World Federation of Neurology states that "[Dyslexia is] a disorder manifested by difficulty in learning to read despite conventional instruction, adequate intelligence, and sociocultural opportunity" (Critchley, 1975).

Some problems with the definition of dyslexia are immediately apparent. What constitutes "normal intelligence"? How *much* difficulty in learning to read and write has to be manifested before a child can be called dyslexic? Researchers studying dyslexia will often adopt a set of criteria such as requiring that a child have a verbal IQ of 90 or over, and a reading age at least 2 years behind that child's actual, chronological age. There should be no obvious visual or hearing impairments, and the child should have had adequate opportunity to learn to read. The emphasis is on identifying children who would normally have been expected to have learnt to read and write without undue difficulty, given their general physical and intellectual endowments and their social and educational background.

But suppose that a child's upbringing has been such that one could legitimately query whether it is reasonable to expect him or her to have learned to read well. In such circumstances, a psychologist may feel that the child is having problems learning to read and write because he or she is genuinely dyslexic and would experience difficulty whatever the child's background, but the psychologist might also harbour the suspicion that the causes of this bright child's failure to learn to read lie in the environment and in the nature of the upbringing the child has experienced. Seen in this light, one can understand why children positively diagnosed as dyslexic tend to be the bright offspring of "good" homes attending "good" schools. There is no reason to suppose that dyslexia is in any real sense a middle-class disease: it is just that those tend to be the cases where psychologists feel most confident they can exclude other obvious causes of reading failure.

Although the World Federation of Neurology definition of dyslexia claims that it is "frequently of constitutional origin", in practice the defining criteria are psychological and social. This means that questions like "How common is dyslexia?" have to be approached with care. To qualify as dyslexic, a child's IQ must be of a certain level, his or her reading age must be below what one would expect from his or her age and IQ, and the home background and education must pass certain minimum requirements. If we chose the criteria of a verbal IQ over 90 and a reading age at least 2 years below chronological age, then a survey of the school population would uncover a certain percentage of children who qualified as "dyslexic" (perhaps around 2–4%). However, if we adopt more stringent criteria and require a verbal IQ of 110 or above and a reading age 30 months below chronological age, then the percentage of apparently dyslexic children would decrease dramatically.

Dyslexia is not a disease like measles which a person can be clearly diagnosed as either having or not having. There is a gradient from good through average to very poor reading, and it is largely arbitrary where one draws the line and says that children below this line are candidates for the label "dyslexic" (only candidates because other causes of poor reading still have to be ruled out). If one is looking for a medical analogy, then obesity may be better than measles (Ellis, 1985). People range from painfully thin through average to very fat, but it is to a considerable degree arbitrary where the line is drawn that separates the obese from the non-obese. That fact does not invalidate the concept of obesity, nor does it prevent good research being carried out into its causes. Similarly, acknowledging that there is a continuum from good reading to dyslexic reading does not invalidate the concept of dyslexia or prevent its causes being sought. What it should do, however, is to make us suspicious of claims that so many per cent of children in school are dyslexic, because a simple change of criteria can radically change that percentage without anything having changed out there in the real world.

THE COGNITIVE BASIS OF DYSLEXIA

The World Federation of Neurology definition mentions "fundamental cognitive disabilities" of possible "constitutional origin". The quest for those disabilities and their origins in the constitution of the individual has preoccupied most of the researchers who have been drawn into the study of dyslexia. Because reading is not a natural skill and has only spread into the general population in very recent times, there can be no faults in our genetic make-up or deficiencies in the pattern of cognitive skills we are born with that are in any way *specific* to reading and writing. If fundamental cognitive deficiencies underlie dyslexia, they must be deficiencies in cognitive abilities which are required for the acquisition of reading and writing but are themselves of a more general nature and application.

Deficits in a whole list of cognitive skills, including visual processing, phonological awareness and short-term memory, have been proposed from time to time as *the* fundamental deficit in dyslexia. But if dyslexia has a single cause, one might expect all dyslexics to show the same pattern of difficulties when it comes to processing print. If dyslexics are *not* all alike in their reading and writing, then one might suspect that different deficiencies underlie the different forms of dyslexia. After all, it would not be surprising if the acquisition of a skill as complex as reading could be derailed by more than one fundamental cognitive deficiency. Before we tackle the question of what cognitive deficiencies underlie dyslexia, we must therefore tackle the question of whether there are significant individual differences between children who meet the criteria for classification as dyslexic.

Individual Differences in Dyslexia

Many psychologists who have worked with dyslexic children have come to the view that dyslexics are not all alike, but differ one from another in ways that need to be described and explained. A variety of approaches have been adopted to the issue of how best to capture those individual differences between dyslexics. Broadly speaking, the approaches to individual differences can be placed in one of two camps (Ellis, 1985). The first approach differentiates between dyslexics in terms of the other cognitive problems that accompany poor reading. For example, Mattis and his colleagues identified a group of children who met the standard criteria for dyslexia, and then attempted to classify them in terms of the additional problems they had (Mattis, 1981; Mattis, French, & Rapin, 1975). The largest sub-group, accounting for some 60% of their dyslexics, was the "language disorder group". These were children who, in addition to their dyslexia, had problems with object naming, speech sound discrimination, and both the comprehension and repetition of spoken sentences. But in addition there were smaller sub-groups whose problems were characterised as having to do with phoneme sequencing, articulatory and motor co-ordination, or visuo-spatial perception. About 10% of dyslexics could not be classified easily because of the multiple and widespread nature of their difficulties.

This approach may have its uses, but because it fails to analyse reading and writing performance in any detail, one cannot tell exactly how these wider cognitive difficulties relate to the pattern of reading and writing problems that an individual dyslexic may show. The alternative approach to individual differences focuses on differences in the strengths and weaknesses of the various component processes involved in reading. If reading and writing are multi-component skills, involving sub-skills such as letter identification, word recognition and production, semantic access, and so on, then one can ask whether dyslexics differ in the extent to which these sub-skills are relatively intact or deficient. This is, of course, the approach to describing and explaining the acquired dyslexias that was reviewed in Chapter 4.

Several psychologists working on developmental dyslexia have been intrigued by the notion that there may be parallels to be drawn between varieties of developmental dyslexia and the varieties of acquired dyslexia that can be seen following brain injury in adulthood. Though one may doubt the wisdom of drawing simple parallels between the two forms of reading difficulty, it is worth noting that this is not a new idea: Hinshelwood (1917) entitled his book *Congenital Word-blindness* precisely to highlight the parallel with acquired word-blindness, as acquired dyslexia was then known. Comparisons between developmental and acquired dyslexia should, however, be made with great care. For example, one might expect on purely theoretical grounds that the cognitive deficits in developmental dyslexia will be broader than those seen in acquired dyslexia. Also, acquired dyslexias are explained in terms of models of skilled, adult word recognition, whereas the appropriate framework for understanding developmental dyslexia may be theories of normal reading development of the sort we encountered in the previous chapter (see Frith, 1985; Snowling, 1987).

Developmental Phonological Dyslexia

Temple and Marshall (1983) reported the case of a 17-year-old developmental dyslexic girl, H.M., who they described as a "developmental phonological dyslexic". We saw in Chapter 4 that acquired phonological dyslexics rely to a very large extent on whole-word recognition of written words. They have impaired phonological reading skills, and so are very poor at reading aloud unfamiliar words or nonwords. They show no advantage in reading regular words as compared with irregular words, because they read all words as wholes and cannot take advantage of the opportunity for sublexical letter–sound conversion afforded by words with regular spellings. The real-word reading of acquired phonological dyslexics is not, however, perfect. In particular, they are prone to visual errors when reading single words aloud.

H.M.'s reading showed a very similar pattern. Her IQ, memory span and command of the spoken language were quite normal, but her reading age was only around 10 or 11 years. Her reading of unfamiliar words and nonwords was very poor. When shown 10 very simple three-letter nonwords, she misread 4 of them (GOK read as "joke", BIX as "back", NUP as "nap" and HIB as "hip"). Her errors to nonwords were typically visually similar real words, indicating that she tried to use her whole-word recognition procedures to read unfamiliar words. She was no better at reading regular words than irregular words and made visual errors to both (e.g. reading CHEERY as "cherry" and BOUQUET as "boutique").

Temple and Marshall (1983) did not explore to any great extent H.M.'s strengths and weaknesses in tasks that involve phonological processing but not reading or writing—tasks such as those described in the previous chapter as tests of "phonological awareness". A series of papers by Snowling, Hulme and colleagues have provided us with a broader description of the cognitive abilities of a developmental phonological dyslexic, J.M., who has been followed over a period of several years (Hulme & Snowling, 1992; Snowling & Hulme, 1989; Snowling, Stackhouse, & Rack, 1986; Snowling, Hulme, Wells, & Goulandris, 1992). J.M. was first reported as an 8½-year-old, when he formed part of a small group of dyslexics studied by Snowling et al. (1986). The most recent account available at the time of writing takes him up to the age of 13 years 4 months.

At the age of 8 years 5 months, J.M.'s IQ was measured at 123 (in the "superior" range). One would expect a child of that age and IQ to have a reading age above 9 years, but in fact J.M.'s reading age was only around 7 years. His spelling was even worse, being down at the level of a normal 6½-year-old. J.M. was able to read 37% of a set of real words but none of a set of nonwords, though younger normal children with the same reading age as J.M. could read 50% of the nonwords.

By the age of 12 years 2 months, J.M.'s reading age had advanced to somewhere between 9 and 10 years (depending on the test used), and his spelling to the level of a 9-year-old. J.M. could now read 84% of the words that he could only read 37% of before, and his nonword reading had begun to register on the scale. In fact, he could now read 26% of the nonwords that had previously defeated him completely. However, normal control subjects matched to J.M.'s current reading age of 9–10 years could read an average of 91% of the nonwords, so J.M.'s phonological, sublexical reading was still very poor, despite his having received what Snowling and Hulme (1989) describe as "intensive and specialist teaching".

J.M.'s visual memory (e.g. memory for meaningless shapes) proved to be normal, but his performance on many phonological tasks was poor. These included word and nonword repetition, and short-term memory for sequences of words or digits. Although he is described as a lively speaker and good conversationalist, he was less fluent than would be expected of someone of his age and intelligence, and had difficulty articulating long words and words containing consonant clusters. His picture naming was also poor for his age, suggesting problems in the storage and/or retrieval of spoken words.

J.M. was not, however, equally impaired on all tasks that one might think of as assessing phonological ability or awareness. For example, although he had difficulty repeating nonwords, he was good at classifying pairs of spoken nonwords as same or different, even when the differences were minimal. Hulme and Snowling (1992) suggest that J.M. had problems with *output* phonology (storing, retrieving and producing spoken word-forms), rather than with input phonology (perceiving and comprehending speech). In terms of Fig. 3.1, J.M. had a deficit which affected the development of his speech output lexicon and phoneme level.

These problems caused him to have some word-finding difficulties in speaking and some problems with articulation, but not enough to prevent him participating in conversations. However, the speech output lexicon and the phoneme level play such crucial roles in the development of reading and spelling (both whole-word and sublexical) that deficits in their functioning greatly retarded the normal acquisition of literacy.

Before we move on to other forms of developmental dyslexia, two more cases of developmental phonological dyslexia deserve a passing mention, if only because they are both people who overcame their difficulties to the point where they were able to attend university and compete at a high academic level. Campbell and Butterworth (1985) report the case of a young woman, R.E., who was an undergraduate at the University of London. What drew her to the attention of psychologists was her inability to read the new words she came across in the course of her studies. Closer analysis revealed a developmental phonological dyslexic pattern, with reasonably good reading of real words and very poor reading of nonwords. R.E. was also poor on phonological tests that required neither reading nor writing. It will come as no surprise to those with experience of dyslexia to learn that R.E. had struggled at school and had become a "behaviour problem". Phonic teaching methods were tried with little success, but with her mother's help she painstakingly acquired a sight vocabulary. Though she could not read new words aloud, she continued to teach herself to associate the appearance of new words with their meanings and pronunciations on a whole-word basis as she came across them. That is, she created entries for words in her visual input lexicon, semantic system and speech output lexicon, and formed associations between those representations, though she could not form the associations between letters and sounds that would allow her to sound out new words. R.E. had a difficult educational experience, but she battled against her problems and graduated with an honours degree in psychology.

Funnell and Davison (1989) studied a 35-year-old woman, Louise, who despite being a teacher herself, had a history of problems with reading and writing. Once again, Louise showed the typical phonological dyslexic pattern of reasonably good reading of real words but very poor reading of nonwords, and once again she was poor at phonological tasks that did not involve reading. What is fascinating about this case is that Louise enrolled on a Reading and Language Studies course which required her to learn to use the International Phonetic Alphabet. That is an alphabet used by linguists in which there is one letter for each sound (phoneme) in the language and one sound for each letter. Every spoken word has only one possible spelling in the International Phonetic Alphabet, and each word written in that alphabet has only one possible pronunciation. Contrary to expectations, Louise proved remarkably adept at reading and writing with the International Phonetic Alphabet. She could even read and write nonwords in that alphabet when her performance with the same nonwords using conventional English spelling was very poor.

What could be going on here? We cannot travel back in time to test Louise as a child, but we do know that her childhood was plagued by intermittent hearing loss caused by sinus and middle ear infections. It could be that her hearing problems in some way prevented a range of phonological skills from developing normally and also caused her to rely on visual, whole-word reading processes rather than sublexical, phonological reading. She built up a substantial visual input lexicon but little in the way of letter–sound conversion skills. As an adult, when she was presented with an unfamiliar word or nonword, she often read it as a familiar word (e.g. reading TROST as "toast"). Her visual reading was developed to such a degree that it tended to "capture" attempts to read even what she knew were nonwords. Her visual input lexicon seems to have responded to unfamiliar words and nonwords with the most similar-looking word in her vocabulary, and she seems to have been unable to suppress that tendency. When, however, she encountered the International Phonetic Alphabet with its mixture of familiar and strange letter shapes, the strangeness of the written word-forms seems to have prevented lexical capture and to have allowed her to develop for the first time some phonological reading skills.

Like R.E., Louise graduated successfully from her university course. These case studies should not be interpreted as showing that within every struggling dyslexic there lurks a potential university graduate. What they *do* show, however, is that there are *some* dyslexics whose basic intelligence is of the required level and who have the necessary persistence to overcome, or find ways around, their dyslexia. Documenting their success may help convince other intelligent dyslexics, and those who teach them, that their problems are not insurmountable and that they can go a long way towards attaining their potential despite their dyslexia.

Developmental Surface Dyslexia

Acquired surface dyslexics lean heavily on phonological letter–sound conversion procedures when attempting to read aloud. As a result, they read regular words reasonably well but tend to regularise irregular words (for example, misreading ISLAND as "izland" and BROAD as "brode"). Holmes (1973; 1978) observed similar regularisation errors in four developmental dyslexics and speculated about possible similarities between developmental dyslexia and acquired surface dyslexia.

This comparison was taken further by Coltheart et al. (1983) in their account of a "developmental surface dyslexic" girl. The girl in question, C.D., was of normal intelligence (verbal IQ 105, performance IQ 101), had a normal upbringing and education, had entirely normal speech production and comprehension, no marked defect in short-term memory, and no evidence of any form of neurological abnormality. Nevertheless, at the age of 15 her reading age was only between 10 and 11 years. When given a set of regular and irregular words to read aloud, she read 35 out of 39 regular words correctly but only 26 out of 39 irregular words. This advantage of regular over irregular words is not seen in developmental phonological dyslexia, and suggests a contribution of sublexical letter–sound conversion to her reading. Many of C.D.'s errors were regularisations of irregular words (e.g. reading QUAY as "kway", COME as "kome" and BEAR as "beer").

It should be noted, however, that C.D.'s reading of nonwords was not as good as one might have expected in a 15-year-old girl whose reading of words showed an influence of sublexical letter–sound conversion. For example, she read only 12 of 50 three- to five-letter single-syllable nonwords correctly, tending to read many of them as visually similar real words. One might suggest on the basis of this that although C.D. and Holmes's dyslexics *tried* to read phonologically, their phonological reading ability was still not terribly good (Wilding, 1989).

Better phonological ability in the context of surface dyslexic reading was shown by a 22-year-old man, Allan, reported by Hanley, Hastie, and Kay (1991). After initially being regarded by his teachers as a "slow learner", Allan was properly assessed at the age of 12 and classified as dyslexic. He left school at the age of 16 to train as a motor mechanic, though his problems (particularly his spelling difficulties) made progress on a 2-year course in motor vehicle technology difficult. Although he had a verbal IQ of 122 and a performance IQ of 133, and was head mechanic in a city garage by the age of 22, it was felt that his reading and writing problems could well be a barrier to further advancement.

Like C.D. and the acquired surface dyslexics, Allan was better at reading regular words aloud than irregular words, which he tended to regularise. Examples of his reading errors include BIND read as "binned", QUICHE as "kwish" and SCENE as "sken". He also made visual errors such as reading BOUQUET as "boutique" and AUDIENCE as "ordinance". But unlike C.D., Allan's reading of nonwords was normal. Thus, he read 27 out of 30 nonwords correctly, compared with 26 out of 30 real words of similar length and complexity. He also scored well on tests of phonological ability that did not involve reading or writing (for example, repeating words and nonwords, judging whether or not spoken words rhyme, and counting phonemes in words). Thus, Allan seems to represent a fairly pure case of a developmental surface dyslexic who had good phonological skills and good sublexical reading, but whose difficulty learning to recognise words as wholes prevented him from becoming a fluent reader and created particular problems when it came to reading irregular words. In terms of Fig. 3.1, "difficulty learning to recognise words as wholes" presumably means difficulty in establishing and retaining entries within the visual input lexicon.

The Nature of Dyslexic Variability

Previous investigators have made proposals for subdividing dyslexics into categories that resemble developmental phonological and surface dyslexia. For example, Boder (1971; 1973) drew a distinction between what she termed dysphonetic and dyseidetic dyslexia. *Dysphonetic* dyslexics are of the "phonological" type, possessing a limited sight vocabulary of words which they are able to recognise visually, but are very poor at phonic decoding. According to Boder, the errors of dysphonetic dyslexics are often visual, e.g. reading HOUSE as "horse", MONEY as "monkey" or STEP as "stop". *Dyseidetic* dyslexics are of the "surface" type. According to Boder (1973, p. 670), the dyseidetic dyslexic "reads laboriously, as if he is seeing each word for the first time ... He is an analytic reader and reads 'by ear', through a process of phonetic analysis and synthesis, sounding out familiar as well as unfamiliar combinations of letters." Typical errors of the dyseidetic dyslexic are regularisations such as BUSINESS read as "bussyness" or TALK as "talc". Mitterer (1982) drew a similar distinction between "whole-word" (phonological) and "recoding" poor readers.

Less extreme versions of developmental phonological and surface dyslexia were encountered in the previous chapter, but there we called them "Chinese" and "Phoenecian" readers (after Baron & Strawson, 1986). "Chinese" readers, it will be recalled, are children (or adults) whose reading is reasonably normal for their age but who lean heavily on visual whole-word recognition and show poor phonic skills, while "Phoenecian" readers are children or adults whose reading is reasonably normal for their age but who lean heavily on phonic letter–sound conversion. Chinese and Phoenecians form two ends of a continuum, with most readers lying somewhere in between, having a reasonable competence in both whole-word recognition and phonic reading. If the same were true of developmental dyslexics, then developmental phonological dyslexics like J.M. and developmental surface dyslexics like Allan would represent two ends of a spectrum with most dyslexics lying somewhere between. If so, then one would not expect to be able to classify dyslexics into a small number of sub-types in any simple manner: some dyslexics would look like relatively pure phonological dyslexics and others like relatively pure surface dyslexics, but most would show features of both.

Wilding (1989) came to this conclusion after a careful review of the cases in the literature and was reinforced in his view by an in-depth study of six new cases (Wilding, 1990). Seymour (1990) came to the same conclusion following an analysis of a number of dyslexics he had studied closely and reported in a series of papers (e.g. Seymour, 1986; 1987; 1990; Seymour & MacGregor, 1984). Although some dyslexics come close to the "pure" phonological or "pure" surface types, most show traces of both. It would make the life of researchers easier if dyslexics fell neatly and tidily into a small number of different sub-types, but they do not, and any attempt to force them into mutually exclusive categories distorts the nature of dyslexic reality.

Are There Other Forms of Developmental Dyslexia?

Even if one accepts a phonological–surface continuum (rather than a neat dichotomy), is it still the case that we can place all dyslexics somewhere on that continuum? We know that there is more to acquired dyslexia than could ever be captured by a phonological–surface continuum: for example, the semantic errors made by acquired deep dyslexics sets them apart from both phonological and surface dyslexics. Jorm (1979) argued for a general similarity between developmental dyslexia and acquired deep dyslexia. This comparison soon ran into difficulties, however (Baddeley, Ellis, Miles, & Lewis, 1982; Ellis, 1979). For example, out-and-out semantic errors seldom, if ever, occur in the reading of most developmental dyslexics. However, Johnston (1983) reported the case of an 18-year-old girl, C.R., whose reading age was only 6 years 2 months. Like acquired deep dyslexics, C.R. was better reading imageable than abstract nouns and was extremely poor at reading nonwords. Over the course of several sessions, C.R. was given 382 words to read aloud. She read 78 correctly and was unable to offer any response to a further 219 words. Fifty of C.R.'s errors were classified as visual errors (e.g. CIGAR read as "sugar", COST as "cot" and RICE as "ripe"). Among her other errors were five errors classified as semantic (OFFICE read as "occupation", DOWN as "up", SEVEN as "eight", CHAIR as "table" and TABLE as "chair").

C.R. may have been a genuine developmental deep dyslexic, but one would ideally like to see a case showing a higher incidence of semantic errors to single words. Also, C.R. suffered from a head injury when young, and one cannot be as confident as one would like to be that no brain injury occurred. Siegel (1985) reported six other children who appear to have made semantic errors to words presented in isolation, but it remains puzzling that there are not more accounts of semantic errors being made by developmental dyslexics in response to single words when many psychologists would undoubtedly appreciate the significance of such errors. Developmental deep dyslexia may exist, but if it does it would appear to be rare. The great majority of children who meet the standard criteria for being called dyslexic are not developmental deep dyslexics.

There may be yet other forms of developmental dyslexia awaiting proper description. For example, Ciuffreda, Bahill, Kenyon, and Stark (1976) discuss the case of an individual with deficient eye movement control who, unsurprisingly, experienced great difficulty with reading. Hinshelwood (1917, pp. 49–51) describes a dyslexic boy whose symptoms bear more than a passing resemblance to acquired letter-by-letter reading. If the multi-component approach to the reading skill that we have adopted in this book is valid, it would certainly not be surprising if more forms of developmental dyslexia exist. Deficits to any one of the many cognitive processes involved in reading could cause an otherwise intelligent child to experience difficulties learning to read. But only when we have a greater wealth of detailed studies describing distinct patterns of dyslexic breakdown will we know what those different forms are.

IS THERE ANYTHING SPECIAL ABOUT BEING DYSLEXIC?

Psychologists who study dyslexia go to a great deal of trouble to assemble a group of individuals with unexpected reading problems; that is, a group of individuals of normal or above-average intelligence whose reading, despite adequate educational opportunities, falls well below expected levels of competence. Recently, however, a growing number of voices have been heard to query whether the reading characteristics of this carefully assembled group differ in any important ways from those of normal individuals performing at the same general level of reading ability. Several studies have now been published in which dyslexics are compared against normal control children who are matched on reading age (and are therefore younger than the dyslexics). Some studies find no difference, implying that although dyslexics are struggling to learn to read, their pattern of reading at a particular stage of development is like that of non-dyslexics at the same stage (e.g. Beech & Harding, 1984; Treiman & Hirsh-Pasek, 1985). More studies, however, find a difference between dyslexics and reading age controls (Rack, Snowling, & Olson, 1992; Stanovich, 1991). In particular, dyslexics have been reported to be worse at nonword reading than reading age controls (e.g. Kochnower, Richardson, & DiBenedetto, 1983; Snowling, 1980). Rack et al. (1992) discuss several reasons why different studies may have produced different results. But given that reading ages are assigned on the basis of a child's ability to read real words aloud, the results of those studies which find a nonword reading deficit imply that the phonological problems experienced by the majority of developmental dyslexics result in dyslexics as a group being worse at sublexical (phonic) reading than non-dyslexics whose reading of real words is comparable to theirs.

A related issue is whether the individual differences that we know to exist between developmental dyslexics are any greater or in any way different from those we know to exist between normal readers. Bryant and Impey (1986) began an investigation into this issue by noting that Temple and Marshall's (1983) developmental phonological dyslexic H.M. and Coltheart and co-workers' developmental surface dyslexic C.D. both had reading ages of 10 or 11. Bryant and Impey tested 16 ordinary children of the same reading age as H.M. and C.D. on regular and irregular words, homophones and nonwords, and claimed to find non-dyslexic children with very similar patterns to H.M. and C.D. In other words, developmental phonological dyslexics resemble younger normal "Chinese" readers, while developmental surface dyslexics resemble younger normal "Phoenecian" readers.

Studies comparing dyslexics with younger non-dyslexics of the same reading age are still thin on the ground. Even thinner are studies comparing dyslexics with children of the same chronological age and the same reading age whose reading is not *unexpectedly* poor. If there is one dyslexic in a class of 12-year-olds who has an IQ of 120 but a reading age of 10, there will be several more children whose reading age is also 10 but whose IQ is such that a reading age of 10 is only to be expected. Do the reading abilities of intelligent dyslexics differ from those of the other poor readers in the same class?

This is an important question because dyslexics are singled out for special attention partly on the basis of an implicit assumption that they need to be treated differently from ordinary poor readers. Yet as Stanovich (1991) observes, remarkably few studies have put this assumption to the test. Ellis and Large (1987) compared a group of dyslexics with a group of good readers of similar IQ and also with a group of ordinary poor readers with lower IQs than the dyslexics. The dyslexics differed from their better reading peers on phonological tasks, short-term memory and naming skills, but these factors did not discriminate dyslexics from ordinary poor readers. The only tasks to do that successfully were visual tasks such as finding hidden objects in pictures and assembling jigsaw-like puzzles, on which the dyslexics did better than the poor readers. This presumably reflected the higher performance IQs of the dyslexics.

Siegel (1989) claims that although poor readers fare consistently badly on tests of phonological and orthographic processing, these effects are independent of IQ; that is, they are no more prominent in high IQ (dyslexic) poor readers than low IQ (ordinary) poor readers. Other studies have found differences between dyslexics and ordinary poor readers (e.g. Aaron, 1987), so we cannot yet provide a firm answer to the question of how, if at all, dyslexics differ from their poor reading classmates. Psychologists tend to find dyslexics fascinating precisely because their reading problems *are* unexpected. The reading difficulties of ordinary poor readers are predictable and for that reason may attract less interest.

THE BIOLOGICAL BASIS OF DYSLEXIA

It is been widely assumed that something in the biological make-up of dyslexics makes them the way they are. In a sense, this is inevitable: If a group of children has good general intelligence, adequate vision and hearing, adequate homes and schooling and has no apparent emotional blockage, then there is little left to retard their reading other than a weakness that they brought into the world with them. That said, good evidence for a biological basis of dyslexia has been a long time coming.

One line of evidence has come from studies of the inheritance of reading problems. Vogler, DeFries, and Decker (1985) found that children of parents with reading problems were significantly more likely to have reading problems themselves than the children of parents without reading problems. It is, of course, possible that reading problems run in families for social or environmental reasons. The stronger evidence that pins such effects to genetics rather than the environment comes from studies comparing the co-occurrence of reading problems in identical twins with their co-occurrence in non-identical twins and other family members. Olson et al. (1990) found that variation in phonological ability of the sort required to segment phonemes in spoken words or read nonwords was highly heritable. Word-specific reading processes of the sort required to indicate which of PEAR or PAIR is a fruit were not heritable. Thus it would appear that some children inherit a phonological problem that can in some cases be fairly specific in nature. The result is a child with good general cognitive skills but a weakness in a particular aspect of language that is crucial for the acquisition of reading and writing. In pre-literate societies, such children might pass unnoticed (just as children with very poor spatial ability do in our society), but this minor cognitive deficit can have devastating consequences in a society that expects universal literacy.

In most people, the left hemisphere of the brain is responsible for language processes. Certain areas within the left hemisphere of the brain are known to be particularly involved in language processing and are typically larger than the corresponding areas in the non-linguistic right hemisphere. One such area is the *planum temporale*. Galaburda and colleagues measured the size of the left and right planum temporales in a small number of dyslexic brains and reported that the usual asymmetry in size was lacking (Galaburda & Kemper, 1979; Galaburda et al., 1985). More recent studies have lent support to this claim using data obtained by non-invasive scanning of the brains of living dyslexics (Hynd et al., 1990; Larsen, Hoien, Lundberg, & Odegaard, 1990). Once again, the planum temporales of dyslexics were found to be similar in size in the two hemispheres, whereas the one on the left was larger in the dyslexics.

The planum temporale forms part of Wernicke's area, which is known to play a part in phonological processing. There are, however, reasons why we should be cautious and not proclaim the discovery of the "dyslexia area" too soon. For a start, some non-dyslexics turn out to have symmetrical planum temporales. If developmental dyslexics are not all alike, we should not expect them all to show the same neurological abnormalities. It may also be the case that the dyslexics involved in these studies have had more severe reading and writing problems than most of the dyslexics who become involved in less invasive cognitive investigations.

Finally, Rumsey and his colleagues (1987) found increases in blood flow in the left hemispheres of a group of right-handed adult dyslexics during reading tasks, indicative of increases in activity levels within that hemisphere. This implies that reading in most developmental dyslexics, like reading in most other people, is mediated by the left hemisphere of the brain, but that this hemisphere operates inefficiently.

SPELLING AND WRITING IN DYSLEXIA

The difficulties that developmental dyslexics experience in spelling and writing are often at least as severe, if not worse, than their difficulties in reading. It is said that persistent spelling problems often give away the adult dyslexic whose reading has, by dint of painful drill and practice, attained a reasonable level of competence (Miles, 1983). This may be because more time is spent working on reading than on spelling, or it may be that spelling problems can be more resistant to remediation than reading problems.

We have noted that the reading of some developmental dyslexics is characterised by particular difficulty with phonics, while others have particular difficulty with whole-word reading. Most have problems with both, but it is of interest to discover whether the spelling and writing of those dyslexics with a particular phonological or lexical problem in reading matches their reading profile. The indications are that it does (Temple, 1986).

Developmental phonological dyslexics can gradually learn to spell words, but they do this on a whole-word basis. Their spelling of nonwords is as bad as their reading of nonwords, implying that their underlying phonological problems retard the learning of correspondences between letters and phonemes in both directions (letters to phonemes in reading; phonemes to letters in spelling). The spelling errors of developmental phonological dyslexics are seldom "phonetic" (i.e. seldom sound like the target word), but often contain several of the right letters, even when those are letters in irregular words which cannot be predicted on the basis of their pronunciation (Seymour & Porpodas, 1980). Examples are H.M. misspelling "daughter" as DORGHER and "chorus" as CHORCE (Temple & Marshall, 1983), and Campbell and Butterworth's (1985) phonological dyslexic student R.E. misspelling "phlegm" as PHELMN and "gymkhana" as GYMGANHA. In Chapter 6, we attributed similar errors in normal spellers to their having incomplete representations of the spellings of some words in their graphemic output lexicons. The same diagnosis may hold for these developmental phonological dyslexics.

Developmental surface dyslexics try to read phonologically using sublexical letter–sound correspondences. Their spelling shows a similar pattern. They try to spell on the basis of the sounds of words, and hence have particular problems with irregular words and make phonic errors. Examples of this are C.D. misspelling "search" as SURCH and "familiar" as FERMILLYER (Coltheart et al., 1983), and Allan misspelling "shoe" as SHOO, "quiche" as KEASH and "knee" as NEA (Hanley et al., 1991).

Finally, developmental dyslexics usually write poorly in the sense of showing poor execution of even those words which can be spelled correctly. Descriptions and samples of dyslexic handwriting can be found in Orton (1931), Hermann and Voldby (1946) and Critchley and Critchley (1978). Hermann and Voldby note among other things the similarity between certain characteristic dyslexic errors, such as the tendency to fuse adjacent letters into one, and some of the types of slip of the pen observed in normal adults. This may be one of those many cases where a dysfunction shows itself as a heightened tendency to errors which normal people are also prone to make at a much lower rate.

TEACHING DYSLEXICS

A condition can be inherited and yet still respond to treatment. Unfortunately, although much effort is expended on trying to teach dyslexics to read and write, there have been few systematic studies of the effects of remedial teaching.

The teaching methods used with dyslexics tend to place great emphasis on phonics (Hornsby, 1985; Naidoo, 1981). That is, they are directed at what is for many dyslexics the greatest area of difficulty. Several studies have shown that dyslexics *can* make reasonable progress when given systematic instruction (e.g. Andrews & Shaw, 1986; Lovett, Ransby, & Barron, 1988; Thomson, 1988), but the dyslexics in these studies are usually engaging in all sorts of reading-related activities. That, and the frequent absence of appropriate control groups, means that it is very difficult to know just what helps most and what does not help at all.

In the previous chapter, it was suggested that a reader who acquires a reasonable grasp of phonics is in a better position to make progress because he or she will have a chance of identifying words encountered in print for the first time. The reader lacking phonics can only guess or ask. But we noted earlier that Campbell and Butterworth's (1985) dyslexic student R.E. apparently made little progress when taught phonically and had resorted to whole-word methods to build up her sight vocabulary. It may be that there are some dyslexics whose phonological deficits are so severe that no amount of teaching will enable them to develop and use sublexical letter–sound correspondences.

We do not know whether the progress made by dyslexics under phonic tuition relates to their underlying degree of phonological deficit, nor do we know whether what works best for developmental phonological dyslexics also works best for dyslexics at the surface end of the continuum. For that matter, as Stanovich (1991) observes, we do not know whether the prognosis for dyslexics differs from that of the ordinary poor readers in the same class, and we do not know whether they need different treatment from ordinary poor readers. Given all the work that *has* been done on dyslexia, these are lamentable gaps in our knowledge that urgently need to be filled.

DEVELOPMENTAL COMPREHENSION DISORDERS

Thus far we have been considering children (and adults) who have problems with reading or spelling, but whose understanding of spoken language is good. To the extent that a dyslexic can read a passage of text, he or she will understand that passage as well as any other person of comparable reading ability (Conners & Olson, 1990; Spring & French, 1990). This is clearly shown in case studies of dyslexics with severe reading problems but normal language comprehension (Aaron, Frantz, & Manges, 1990; Snowling & Hulme, 1989).

We can say, then, that dyslexics have problems converting print into speech and vice versa, but that their language comprehension is normal for their age and general ability. There is, however, an under-investigated sub-group of children who show the reverse pattern: children who are good at converting print to sound (i.e. good at reading aloud) but who show poor understanding of what they read. The most extreme form of this is known as *hyperlexia*. Silberberg and Silberberg (1968) described a hyperlexic 9-year-old boy with a measured IQ of only 64 (far below normal) whose expressive speech was poorly developed, but who nevertheless was able to read words to a third-grade (10-year-old) level. Significantly, Silberberg and Silberberg add that, "Of course, his comprehension of what he read was commensurate with his measured intelligence" (p. 5).

The first of three children described by Huttenlocher and Huttenlocher (1973) is a 7-year-old boy (M.K.) with an IQ of only 77 and with speech and motor development equivalent to that of a normal 3½-year-old child. At the age of 2, "he learned nursery rhymes and television commercials with remarkable facility, but he had great difficulty in learning to associate names with objects in picture books" (p. 1108). Between 4 and 4½ years, he learned to read "with minimal parental help" and at the age of 4 years 10 months he is described as having read fluently a passage appropriate for a normal 10-year-old. Healy, Aram, Horowitz, and Kessler (1982) described 12 hyperlexic children, all of whom could read a story aloud almost perfectly, but none of whom could relate anything about the content of what they had just read.

Reading models of the sort represented by Fig. 3.1 predict precisely the dissociation between decoding (reading aloud) and comprehension that is seen when we contrast dyslexics (poor decoding/good comprehension) with hyperlexics (good decoding/poor comprehension). This is because the module responsible for comprehension (the semantic system) is distinct and separate from the various modules involved in converting print to sound (the visual analysis system, the visual input lexicon, the speech output lexicon and the phoneme level). In dyslexics the problem lies with developing those latter modules, whereas in hyperlexics the problem lies with developing the semantic system.

Hyperlexia is an extreme and somewhat uncommon condition. But there is evidence that a milder form of the same pattern—good decoding with poor comprehension—can be seen more commonly in ordinary school children. There are within the normal school population children who appear to learn to read without difficulty (in that they can read aloud fluently and competently), yet they are poor at understanding what they read.

Although we have ascribed poor comprehension in hyperlexia to the semantic system, it does not seem to be the case that poor comprehenders are poor at accessing the meanings of individual words. Yuill and Oakhill (1991) found no difference between good and poor comprehenders in the speed with which they could assign individual written words to different semantic categories. The problem seems to be of a higher order: Poor comprehenders have difficulty combining the meanings of single words into representations of the meanings of phrases, sentences and texts. They draw few inferences from what they read (Oakhill, 1983), and although their memory for the verbatim content of what they have read may be reasonable, they retain little of the gist (Yuill & Oakhill, 1991).

The semantic system of our guiding model is involved in the comprehension of spoken as well as written language. Hence, we would expect children who have disproportionate problems comprehending text also to experience problems in listening comprehension. This appears to be the case. Children who score poorly on tests of reading comprehension also score poorly on listening comprehension tests (Curtis, 1980; Stothard, 1992). Oakhill, Yuill, and Parkin (1986) found that when poor reading comprehenders listened to sentences, they showed the same failure to draw inferences and construct representations of gist that characterise their reading.

Stothard (1992) compared poor comprehenders with younger normal children matched for comprehension skill and found the poor comprehenders to have lower verbal IQs. Their phonological skills were normal for their age, but their language processing was weak whenever sentence and text processing was required. The performance IQs of the poor decoders were normal for their age, however. These are children whose non-verbal intelligence can be very good, and whose language problems do not lie within phonology or the lexicons, but who have linguistic deficits of a more central nature which limit their capacity to understand both spoken and written language.

Teaching strategies aimed at improving the speed and accuracy with which poor comprehenders read aloud fail to improve their understanding of what they read (Perfetti & Hogaboam, 1975; Yuill & Oakhill, 1988). There are, however, other teaching strategies that may help to some degree (Oakhill & Garnham, 1988). One approach is to provide comprehension aids such as pictures or titles. These have been shown to help poor comprehenders understand text (Yuill & Joscelyne, 1988). A second approach is to teach poor comprehenders explicit strategies such as underlining, note-taking or summarising (e.g. Palincsar & Brown, 1984; Paris & Oka, 1986). Although poor comprehenders do not have particular difficulty accessing the meanings of words they already know, their vocabularies are often limited. A third approach works at improving the vocabulary of poor comprehenders. This can result in improved understanding of what they read (Beck, Perfetti, & McKeown, 1982). It must be admitted, though, that the improvements obtained in studies such as these are often relatively modest in comparison with the time and effort put into training the poor comprehenders (Carver, 1987; Pearson & Galagher, 1983).

FURTHER READING

Seymour, P.H.K. (1990). Developmental dyslexia. In M.W. Eysenck (Ed.), *Cognitive psychology: An international review*. Chichester: John Wiley.

Snowling, M. (1987). *Dyslexia: A cognitive developmental perspective*. Oxford: Basil Blackwell.

Snowling, M.J. (1991). Developmental reading disorders. *Journal of Child Psychology and Psychiatry, 32*, 49–77.

Yuill, N. & Oakhill, J. (1991). *Children's problems in text comprehension*. Cambridge: Cambridge University Press.

References

Aaron, P.G. (1987). Developmental dyslexia: Is it different from other forms of reading disability? *Annals of Dyslexia, 37,* 109–125.

Aaron, P.G., Frantz, S.S., & Manges, A.R. (1990). Dissociation between comprehension and pronunciation in dyslexic and hyperlexic children. *Reading and Writing: An Interdisciplinary Journal, 2,* 243–264.

Adams, M.J. (1990). *Beginning to read: Thinking and learning about print.* Cambridge, MA: MIT Press.

Albrow, K.H. (1972). *The English writing system: Notes towards a description.* London: Longmans.

Allport, D.A. (1977). On knowing the meaning of words we are unable to report: The effects of visual masking. In S. Dornic (Ed.), *Attention and performance VI.* Hillsdale, NJ: Lawrence Erlbaum Associates Inc.

Anderson, R.C. & Pichert, J.W. (1978). Recall of previously unrecallable information following a shift in perspective. *Journal of Verbal Learning and Verbal Behaviour, 17,* 1–12.

Andrews, N., & Shaw, J. (1986). The efficacy of teaching dyslexics. *Child: Care, Health and Development, 12,* 53–62.

Ausubel, D.P. (1960). The use of advance organizers in the learning and retention of meaningful verbal material. *Journal of Educational Psychology, 51,* 267–272.

Backman, J., Bruck, M., Hebert, M., & Seidenberg, M.S. (1984). Acquisition and use of spelling–sound correspondences in reading. *Journal of Experimental Child Psychology, 38,* 114–133.

Baddeley, A.D. (1990). *Human memory.* Hove, UK: Lawrence Erlbaum Associates Ltd.

Baddeley, A.D., Ellis, N.C., Miles, T.R., & Lewis, V.J. (1982). Developmental and acquired dyslexia: A comparison. *Cognition, 11,* 185–199.

Baker, R.G. (1980). Orthographic awareness. In U. Frith (Ed.), *Cognitive processes in spelling*. London: Academic Press.

Baron, J. (1979). Orthographic and word-specific mechanisms in children's reading of words. *Child Development, 50,* 60–72.

Baron, J., & Strawson, C. (1976). Use of orthographic and word-specific knowledge in reading aloud. *Journal of Experimental Psychology: Human Perception and Performance, 2,* 386–393.

Baron, J., Treiman, R., Wilf, J.F., & Kellman, P. (1980). Spelling and reading by rules. In U. Frith (Ed.), *Cognitive processes in spelling*. London: Academic Press.

Bartlett, F.C. (1932). *Remembering: A study in experimental and social psychology*. Cambridge: Cambridge University Press.

Beck, I.L., Perfetti, C.A., & McKeown, M.G. (1982). The effects of long–term vocabulary instruction on lexical access and comprehension. *Journal of Educational Psychology, 74,* 506–521.

Becker, C.A. (1979). Semantic context and word frequency effects in visual word recognition. *Journal of Experimental Psychology: Human Perception and Performance, 5,* 252–259.

Becker, C.A., & Killion, T.H. (1977). Interaction of visual and cognitive effects in word recognition. *Journal of Experimental Psychology: Human Perception and Performance, 3,* 389–401.

Beech, J.R., & Harding, L.M. (1984). Phonemic processing and the poor reader from a developmental lag viewpoint. *Reading Research Quarterly, 19,* 357–366.

Besner, D. & Humphreys, G.W. (Eds.). (1991). *Basic processes in reading: Visual word recognition*. Hillsdale, NJ: Lawrence Erlbaum Associates Inc.

Binet, A. & Henri, V. (1894). La mémoire des phrases (mémoire des idées). *L'Année Psychologique, 1,* 24–59.

Bishop, D.V.M. (1990). *Handedness and developmental disorder*. Hove, UK: Lawrence Erlbaum Associates Ltd.

Bissex, G.L. (1980). *GNYS at work: A child learns to write and read*. Cambridge, MA: Harvard University Press.

Bjork, R.A. (1988). Retrieval practice and the maintenance of knowledge. In M.M. Gruneberg, P.E. Morris, & R.N. Sykes (Eds.), *Practical aspects of memory: Current research and issues. Vol. 1: Memory in everyday life*. Chichester: John Wiley.

Boder, E. (1971). Developmental dyslexia: Prevailing diagnostic concepts and a new diagnostic approach. In H.R. Myklebust (Ed.), *Progress in learning disabilities,* Vol. 2. New York: Grune and Stratton.

Boder, E. (1973). Developmental dyslexia: A diagnostic approach based on three atypical reading–spelling patterns. *Developmental Medicine and Child Neurology, 15,* 663–687.

Bond, G.L. & Dykstra, R. (1967). The cooperative research program in first-grade reading instruction. *Reading Research Quarterly, 2,* 5–142.

Bradley, H. (1913). On the relations between spoken and written language with special reference to English. *Proceedings of the British Academy, 6,* 1–22.

Bradley, L. & Bryant, P. (1983). Categorizing sounds and learning to read: A causal connexion. *Nature, 301,* 419.

Bradley, L. & Bryant, P. (1985). *Rhyme and reason in reading and spelling*. Ann Arbor: University of Michigan Press.

Bransford, J.D. & Johnson, M.K. (1972). Contextual prerequisites for understanding: Some investigations of comprehension and recall. *Journal of Verbal Learning and Verbal Behaviour, 11,* 717–726.

Bransford, J.D. & Johnson, M.K. (1973). Consideration of some problems in comprehension. In W. Chase (Ed.), *Visual information processing.* New York: Academic Press.

Brown, G.D.A. & Watson, F.L. (1987). First in, first out: Word learning age and spoken word frequency as predictors of word familiarity and word naming latency. *Memory and Cognition, 15,* 208–216.

Bryant, P. & Bradley, L. (1980). Why children sometimes write words they do not read. In U. Frith (Ed.), *Cognitive processes in spelling.* London: Academic Press.

Bryant, P. & Bradley, L. (1985). *Children's reading problems.* Oxford: Basil Blackwell.

Bryant, P. & Impey, L. (1986). The similarities between normal readers and developmental and acquired dyslexics. *Cognition, 24,* 121–137.

Bub, D. & Kertesz, A. (1982). Deep agraphia. *Brain and Language, 17,* 146–165.

Campbell, R. (1983). Writing nonwords to dictation. *Brain and Language, 19,* 153–178.

Campbell, R. & Butterworth, B. (1985). Phonological dyslexia and dysgraphia in a highly literate subject: A developmental case with associated deficits of phonemic processing and awareness. *Quarterly Journal of Experimental Psychology, 37A,* 435–475.

Carr, T.H., Brown, J.S., & Charalambous, A. (1989). Repetition and reading: Perceptual encoding mechanisms are very abstractive but not very interactive. *Journal of Experimental Psychology: Learning, Memory and Cognition, 15,* 763–778.

Carroll, J.B. & White, M.N. (1973). Word frequency and age-of-acquisition as determiners of picture-naming latency. *Quarterly Journal of Experimental Psychology, 25,* 85–95.

Carver, R.P. (1987). Should reading comprehension skills be taught? In J.E. Readance & R.S. Baldwin (Eds.), *Research in literacy: Merging perspectives.* Rochester, NY: National Reading Conference.

Chall, J.S. (1983). *Learning to read: The great debate* (2nd ed.). New York: McGraw-Hill.

Chomsky, C. (1970). Reading, writing and phonology. *Harvard Educational Review, 40,* 287–309.

Chomsky, N. & Halle, M. (1968). *The sound pattern of English.* New York: Harper and Row.

Ciuffreda, K.J., Bahill, A.T., Kenyon, R.V., & Stark, L. (1976). Eye movements during reading: Case reports. *American Journal of Optometry and Physiological Optics, 53,* 389–395.

Clarke, R.G. & Morton, J. (1983). The effects of priming in visual word recognition. *Quarterly Journal of Experimental Psychology, 35A,* 79–96.

Clay, M. (1985). *The early detection of reading difficulties* (3rd ed.). Tadworth, Surrey: Heinemann.

Clay, M. (1987). Implementing reading recovery: Systematic adaptions to an educational innovation. *New Zealand Journal of Educational Studies, 22,* 35–58.

Collins, A. & Gentner, D. (1980). A framework for a cognitive theory of writing. In L.W. Gregg & E.R. Steinberg (Eds.), *Cognitive processes in writing*. Hillsdale, NJ: Lawrence Erlbaum Associates Inc.

Collins, A.M. & Loftus, E.F. (1975). A spreading-activation theory of semantic processing. *Psychological Review, 82,* 407–408.

Coltheart, M. (1978). Lexical access in simple reading tasks. In G. Underwood (Ed.), *Strategies of information processing*. London: Academic Press.

Coltheart, M. (1979). When can children learn to read—And what should they be taught? In T.G. Waller & G.E. Mackinnon (Eds.), *Reading research: Advances in theory and practice*, Vol. 1. New York: Academic Press.

Coltheart, M. (1980). Deep dyslexia: A right hemisphere hypothesis. In M. Coltheart, K.E. Patterson, & J.C. Marshall (Eds.), *Deep dyslexia*. London: Routledge and Kegan Paul.

Coltheart, M. (1981). Disorders of reading and their implications for models of normal reading. *Visible Language, 15,* 245–286.

Coltheart, M. (1983). The right hemisphere and disorders of reading. In A.W. Young (Ed.), *Functions of the right cerebral hemisphere*. London: Academic Press.

Coltheart, M., Besner, D., Jonasson, J.T., & Davelaar, E. (1979). Phonological encoding in the lexical decision task. *Quarterly Journal of Experimental Psychology, 31,* 489–507.

Coltheart, M., Masterson, J., Byng, S., Prior, M., & Riddoch, J. (1983). Surface dyslexia. *Quarterly Journal of Experimental Psychology, 35A,* 469–495.

Coltheart, M., Patterson, K.E., & Marshall, J.C. (Eds.). (1987). *Deep dyslexia* (2nd ed.). London: Routledge and Kegan Paul.

Coltheart, V., Laxon, V.J., & Keating, C. (1988). Effects of word imageability and age of acquisition on children's reading. *British Journal of Psychology, 79,* 1–12.

Conners, F.A. & Olson, R.K. (1990). Reading comprehension in dyslexic and normal readers: A component skills analysis. In D.B. Balota, G.B. Flores d'Arcais, & K. Rayner (Eds.), *Comprehension processes in reading*. Hillsdale, NJ: Lawrence Erlbaum Associates Inc.

Craik, F.I.M. & Tulving, E. (1975). Depth of processing and the retention of words in episodic memory. *Journal of Experimental Psychology: General, 104,* 268–294.

Critchley, M. (1975). Specific developmental dyslexia. In E.H. Lenneberg & E. Lenneberg (Eds.), *Foundations of language development*, Vol. 2. New York: Academic Press.

Critchley, M. & Critchley, E.R. (1978). *Dyslexia defined*. London: William Heinemann.

Crowder, R.G. (1982). *The psychology of reading: An introduction*. New York: Oxford University Press.

Cunningham, A.E. (1990). Explicit versus implicit instruction in phonemic awareness. *Journal of Experimental Child Psychology, 50,* 429–444.

Curtis, M.E. (1980). Development of components of reading skill. *Journal of Educational Psychology, 72,* 656–669.

Daiute, C.A. (1981). Psycholinguistic foundations of the writing process. *Research in the Teaching of English, 15,* 5–22.

Davis, D.R. & Sinha, D. (1950). The influence of an interpolated experience upon recognition. *Quarterly Journal of Experimental Psychology, 2,* 132–137.

Diringer, D. (1962). *Writing*. London: Thames and Hudson.

Dodge, R. (1900). Visual perception during eye movement. *Psychological Review,* 7, 454–465.

Dole, J.A., Valencia, S.W., Greer, E.A., & Wardrop, J.L. (1991). Effects of two types of prereading instruction on the comprehension of narrative and expository text. *Reading Research Quarterly, 26,* 142–159.

Dooling, D.J. & Lachman, R. (1971). Effects of comprehension on retention of prose. *Journal of Experimental Psychology, 88,* 216–222.

Downing, J. (1973). *Comparative reading*. New York: Macmillan.

Ebbinghaus, H. (1885). *Uber das Gedachtris*. Leipzig: Dunker. (Trans. H. Ruyer & C.E. Bussenius, *Memory*. New York: Teachers College Press, 1913).

Ehri, L.C. (1993). Reconceptualising the development of sight–word reading and its relationship to decoding. In P.B. Gough, L.C. Ehri, & R.Treiman (Eds.), *Reading acquisition*. Hillsdale, NJ: Lawrence Erlbaum Associates Inc.

Ehrlich, S.F. & Rayner, K. (1981). Contextual effects on word perception and eye movements during reading. *Journal of Verbal Learning and Verbal Behavior, 20,* 641–655.

Eichelman, W.H. (1970). Familiarity effects in the simultaneous matching task. *Journal of Experimental Psychology, 86,* 275–282.

Ellis, A.W. (1979). Developmental and acquired dyslexia: Some observations on Jorm (1979). *Cognition, 7,* 413–420.

Ellis, A.W. (1982). Spelling and writing (and reading and speaking). In A.W. Ellis (Ed.), *Normality and pathology in cognitive functions*. London: Academic Press.

Ellis, A.W. (1985). The cognitive neuropsychology of developmental (and acquired) dyslexia: A critical survey. *Cognitive Neuropsychology, 2,* 169–205.

Ellis, A.W. (1988). Normal writing processes and peripheral acquired dysgraphias. *Language and Cognitive Processes, 3,* 99–127.

Ellis, A.W. & Beattie, G. (1986). *The psychology of language and communication*. Hove, UK: Lawrence Erlbaum Associates Ltd.

Ellis, A.W. & Young, A.W. (1988). *Human cognitive neuropsychology*. Hove, UK: Lawrence Erlbaum Associates Ltd.

Ellis, A.W., Flude, B.M., & Young, A.W. (1987). "Neglect dyslexia" and the early visual processing of letters in words and nonwords. *Cognitive Neuropsychology, 4,* 439–464.

Ellis, A.W., Young, A.W., & Flude, B.M. (1987). "Afferent dysgraphia" in a patient and in normal subjects. *Cognitive Neuropsychology, 4,* 465–486.

Ellis, A.W., Young, A.W., & Flude, B.M. (1993). Neglect and visual language. In I.H.Robertson and J.C. Marshall (Eds.), *Unilateral neglect: Clinical and experimental studies*. Hove, UK: Lawrence Erlbaum Associates Ltd.

Ellis, N. & Large, B. (1987). The development of reading: As you seek so shall you find. *British Journal of Psychology, 78,* 1–28.

Evans, M.A. & Carr, T.H. (1985). Cognitive abilities, conditions of learning, and the early development of reading skill. *Reading Research Quarterly, 20,* 327–350.

Eysenck, M.W. & Keane, M.T. (1990). *Cognitive psychology: A student's handbook* (2nd ed.). Hove, UK: Lawrence Erlbaum Associates Ltd.

Fodor, J.A. (1983). *The modularity of mind*. Cambridge, MA: MIT Press.

Forster, K.I. & Chambers, S.M. (1973). Lexical access and naming time. *Journal of Verbal Learning and Verbal Behaviour, 12,* 627–635.

Frith, U. (1978). Spelling difficulties. *Journal of Child Psychology and Psychiatry, 19,* 279–285.

Frith, U. (1980). Unexpected spelling problems. In U. Frith (Ed.), *Cognitive processes in spelling.* London: Academic Press.

Frith, U. (1985). Beneath the surface of developmental dyslexia. In K.E. Patterson, M. Coltheart, & J.C. Marshall (Eds.), *Surface dyslexia: Neuropsychological and cognitive studies of phonological reading.* London: Lawrence Erlbaum Associates Ltd.

Fromkin, V.A. & Rodman, R. (1974). *An introduction to language.* New York: Holt, Rinehart and Winston.

Funnell, E. (1983). Phonological processes in reading: New evidence from acquired dyslexia. *British Journal of Psychology, 74,* 159–180.

Funnell, E. & Davison, M. (1989). Lexical capture: A developmental disorder of reading and spelling. *Quarterly Journal of Experimental Psychology, 41A,* 471–487.

Galaburda, A.M. & Kemper, T.L. (1979). Cytoarchitectonic abnormalities in developmental dyslexia: A case study. *Annals of Neurology, 6,* 94–100.

Galaburda, A.M., Sherman, G.F., Rosen, G.D., Aboitiz, F., & Geschwind, N. (1985). Developmental dyslexia: Four consecutive patients with cortical anomalies. *Annals of Neurology, 18,* 222–233.

Garnham, A. (1985). *Psycholinguistics: Central topics.* London: Methuen

Gaur, A. (1987). *A history of writing.* London: The British Library.

Gelb, I.J. (1963). *A study of writing* (2nd ed.). Chicago: University of Chicago Press.

Geschwind, N. (1982). Why Orton was right. *Annals of Dyslexia, 32,* 13–30.

Gilhooly, K.J. & Logie, R.H. (1981). Word age-of-acquisition, reading latencies and auditory recognition. *Current Psychological Research, 1,* 251–262.

Gilhooly, K.J. & Watson, F.L. (1981). Word age-of-acquisition effects: A review. *Current Psychological Research, 1,* 269–286.

Glushko, R.J. (1979). The organization and activation of orthographic knowledge in reading aloud. *Journal of Experimental Psychology: Human Perception and Performance, 5,* 674–691.

Goswami, U. (1986). Children's use of analogy in learning to read: A developmental study. *Journal of Experimental Child Psychology, 42,* 73–83.

Goswami, U. & Bryant, P. (1990). *Phonological skills and learning to read.* Hove, UK: Lawrence Erlbaum Associates Ltd.

Gough, P.B. (1972). One second of reading. In J.P. Kavanagh & I.G. Mattingly (Eds.), *Language by ear and by eye.* Cambridge, MA: MIT Press.

Gould, J.D. (1978). An experimental study of writing, dictating and speaking. In J. Requin (Ed.), *Attention and performance VII.* Hillsdale, NJ: Lawrence Erlbaum Associates Inc.

Gould, J.D. (1980). Experiments on composing letters: Some facts, some myths, and some observations. In L.W. Gregg & E.R. Steinberg (Eds.), *Cognitive processes in writing.* Hillsdale, NJ: Lawrence Erlbaum Associates Inc.

Gregg, L.W. & Steinberg, E.R. (Eds.). (1980). *Cognitive processes in writing.* Hillsdale, NJ: Lawrence Erlbaum Associates Inc.

Hanley, J.R., Hastie, K., & Kay, J. (1991). Developmental surface dyslexia and dysgraphia: An orthographic processing impairment. *Quarterly Journal of Experimental Psychology, 43A,* 285–310.

Hartley, J. & Davis, I.K. (1976). Preinstructional strategies: The role of pretests, behavioural objectives, overviews and advance organisers. *Review of Educational Research, 46,* 239–265.

Hatcher, P., Hulme, C., & Ellis, A.W. (in press). Ameliorating early reading failure by integrating the teaching of reading and phonological skills: The phonological linkage hypothesis. *Child Development.*

Hatfield, F.M. & Patterson, K.E. (1983). Phonological spelling. *Quarterly Journal of Experimental Psychology, 35,* 451–468.

Hayes, J.R. & Flower, L.S. (1980). Identifying the organisation of the writing process. In L.W. Gregg & E.R. Steinberg (Eds.), *Cognitive processes in writing.* Hillsdale, NJ: Lawrence Erlbaum Associates Inc.

Hayes, J.R. & Flower, L.S. (1986). Writing research and the writer. *American Psychologist, 41,* 1106–1113.

Healy, J.M., Aram, D.M., Horowitz, S.J., & Kessler, J.W. (1982). A study of hyperlexia. *Brain and Language, 17,* 1–23.

Helfgott, J. (1976). Phoneme segmentation and blending skills of kindergarten children: Implications for beginning reading acquisition. *Contemporary Educational Psychology, 1,* 157–169.

Henderson, L. (1982). *Orthography and word recognition in reading.* London: Academic Press.

Hermann, K. & Voldby, H. (1946). The morphology of handwriting in congenital word-blindness. *Acta Psychiatrica et Neurologica, 21,* 349–363.

Hewison, J. (1988). The long–term effectiveness of parental involvement in reading: A follow-up to the Haringey Reading Project. *British Journal of Educational Psychology, 58,* 184–190.

Hinshelwood, J. (1917). *Congenital word-blindness.* London: H.K. Lewis.

Hinton, G.E. & Shallice, T. (1991). Lesioning an attractor network: Investigations of acquired dyslexia. *Psychological Review, 98,* 74–95.

Hofland, K. & Johansson, S. (1988). *Word frequencies in British and American English.* Harlow: Longman.

Holmes, J.M. (1973). *Dyslexia: A neurolinguistic study of traumatic and developmental disorder.* Unpublished PhD thesis, University of Edinburgh.

Holmes, J.M. (1978). "Regression" and reading breakdown. In A. Caramazza & E.B. Zurif (Eds.), *Language acquisition and language breakdown: Parallels and divergences.* Baltimore, MD: Johns Hopkins University Press.

Holmes, M.C. (1928). Investigation of reading readiness of first grade entrants. *Childhood Education, 3,* 215–221.

Hornsby, B. (1985). A structured phonetic-linguistic method for teaching dyslexics. In M.J. Snowling (Ed.), *Children's written language difficulties.* Windsor: NFER-Nelson.

Hotopf, N. (1980). Slips of the pen. In U. Frith (Ed.), *Cognitive processes in spelling.* London: Academic Press.

Hulme, C. & Snowling, M. (1992). Deficits in output phonology: An explanation of reading failure? *Cognitive Neuropsychology, 9,* 47–72.

Humphreys, G.W. & Bruce, V. (1989). *Visual cognition: Computational, experimental and neuropsychological perspectives.* Hove, UK: Lawrence Erlbaum Associates Ltd.

Hunter, I.M.L. (1984). Lengthy verbatim recall (LVR) and the mythical gift of tape-recorder memory. In K. Lagerspetz & P. Niemi (Eds.), *Psychology in the 1990s.* Amsterdam: North–Holland.

Hunter, I.M.L. (1985). Lengthy verbatim recall: The role of text. In A.W. Ellis (Ed.), *Progress in the psychology of language, Vol. 1.* Hove, UK: Lawrence Erlbaum Associates Ltd.

Huttenlocher, P.R. & Huttenlocher, J. (1973). A study of children with hyperlexia. *Neurology, 23,* 1107–1116.

Hynd, G.W., Semrud-Clikeman, M., Lorys, A.R., Novery, E.S., & Eliopulos, D. (1990). Brain morphology in developmental dyslexia and attention deficit disorder/hyperactivity. *Archives of Neurology, 47,* 919–926.

Inhoff, A.W. & Rayner, K. (1986). Parafoveal word processing during eye fixations in reading: Effects of word frequency. *Perception and Psychophysics, 40,* 431–439.

Intons-Peterson, M.J. & Smyth, M.M. (1987). The anatomy of repertory memory. *Journal of Experimental Psychology: Learning, Memory and Cognition, 13,* 490–500.

Jackson, A. & Morton, J. (1984). Facilitation of auditory word recognition. *Memory and Cognition, 12,* 568–574.

Jared, D. & Seidenberg, M.S. (1991). Does word identification proceed from spelling to sound to meaning? *Journal of Experimental Psychology: General, 120,* 358–394.

Johnson, M.K., Bransford, J.D., & Solomon, S.K. (1973). Memory for tacit implications of sentences. *Journal of Experimental Psychology, 98,* 203–205.

Johnson-Laird, P.N. (1987). The mental representation of the meaning of words. *Cognition, 25,* 189–211.

Johnson-Laird, P.N. (1988). *The computer and the mind.* Cambridge, MA: Harvard University Press/London: Fontana.

Johnston, R.S. (1983). Developmental deep dyslexia. *Cortex, 19,* 133–139.

Jorm, A.F. (1979). The cognitive and neurological basis of developmental dyslexia: A theoretical framework and review. *Cognition, 7,* 19–32.

Kay, J. & Marcel, A. (1981). One process, not two, in reading aloud: Lexical analogies do the work of non-lexical rules. *Quarterly Journal of Experimental Psychology, 33A,* 397–413.

Kerr, J. (1896). School hygiene in its mental, moral and physical aspects. *Journal of the Royal Statistical Society, 60,* 613–680.

Kintsch, W. & Keenan (1973). Reading rate and retention as a function of the number of propositions in the base structure of sentences. *Cognitive Psychology, 5,* 257–274.

Kintsch, W. & Kozminsky, E. (1977). Summarising stories after reading and listening. *Journal of Educational Psychology, 69,* 491–499.

Kintsch, W. & van Dijk, T.A. (1978). Towards a model of text comprehension and production. *Psychological Review, 85,* 363–394.

Kochnower, J., Richardson, E., & DiBenedetto, B. (1983). A comparison of the phonic decoding ability of normal and learning disabled children. *Journal of Learning Disabilities, 16,* 348–351.

Kucera, H. & Francis, W. (1967). *Computational analysis of present–day American English.* Providence, RI: Brown University Press.

Larsen, J.P., Hoien, T., Lundberg, I., & Odegaard, H. (1990). MRI evaluation of the size and symmetry of the planum temporale in adolescents with developmental dyslexia. *Brain and Language, 39,* 289–301.

Latour, P.L. (1962). Visual threshold during eye movements. *Vision Research, 2,* 261–262.

Leech, G., Deuchar, M., & Hoogenraad, R. (1982). *English grammar for today.* London: Macmillan.

Levin, H. (1979). *The eye–voice span.* Cambridge, MA: MIT Press.

Levin, H. & Kaplan, E.L. (1970). Grammatical structure and reading. In H. Levin & J.P. Williams (Eds.), *Basic studies on reading.* New York: Basic Books.

Lord, A.B. (1960). *The singer of tales.* Cambridge, MA: Harvard University Press.

Lovett, M., Ransby, M., & Barron, R. (1988). Treatment, subtype and word type in dyslexic children's response to remediation. *Brain and Language, 34,* 328–349.

Lundberg, I., Frost, J., & Peterson, O. (1988). Effects of an extensive program for stimulating phonological awareness in preschool children. *Reading Research Quarterly, 23,* 263–284.

Margolin, D.I. (1984). The neuropsychology of writing and spelling: Semantic, phonological, motor and perceptual processes. *Quarterly Journal of Experimental Psychology, 36A,* 459–489.

Margolin, D.I. & Goodman-Schulman, R. (1992). Oral and written spelling impairments. In D.I. Margolin (Ed.), *Cognitive neuropsychology in clinical practice.* New York: Oxford University Press.

Marsh, G., Friedman, M., Welch, V., & Desberg, P. (1981). A cognitive-developmental theory of reading acquisition. In G.E. Mackinnon & T.G. Waller (Eds.), *Reading research: Advances in theory and practice.* New York: Academic Press.

Marshall, J.C. & Newcombe, F. (1966). Syntactic and semantic errors in paralexia. *Neuropsychologia, 4,* 169–176.

Marshall, J.C. & Newcombe, F. (1973). Patterns of paralexia: A psycholinguistic approach. *Journal of Psycholinguistic Research, 2,* 175–199.

Marshall, J.C. & Newcombe, F. (1980). The conceptual status of deep dyslexia: An historical perspective. In M. Coltheart, K. Patterson, & J. Marshall (Eds.), *Deep dyslexia.* London: Routledge and Kegan Paul.

Mattis, S. (1981). Dyslexia syndromes in children: Toward the development of syndrome-specific treatment programs. In F.J. Pirozzolo & M.C. Wittrock (Eds.), *Neuropsychological and cognitive processes in reading.* New York: Academic Press.

Mattis, S., French, J.H., & Rapin, I. (1975). Dyslexia in children and young adults: Three independent neuropsychological syndromes. *Developmental Medicine and Child Neurology, 17,* 150–163.

McCann, R.S. & Besner, D. (1987). Reading pseudohomophones: Implications for models of pronunciation assembly and the locus of frequency effects in naming. *Journal of Experimental Psychology: Human Perception and Performance, 13,* 13–24.

McCarthy, R.A. & Warrington, E.K. (1990). *Cognitive neuropsychology: A clinical introduction.* San Diego, CA: Academic Press.

McClelland, J.L. & Rumelhart, D.E. (1981). An interactive activation model of context effects in letter perception: Part 1. An account of basic findings. *Psychological Review, 88,* 375–407.

Meyer, D.E. & Schvaneveldt, R.W. (1971). Facilitation in recognizing pairs of words: Evidence of a dependence between retrieval operations. *Journal of Experimental Psychology, 90,* 227–234.

Miceli, G., Silveri, C., & Caramazza, A. (1985). Cognitive analysis of a case of pure dysgraphia. *Brain and Language, 25,* 187–121.

Miceli, G., Silveri, C., & Caramazza, A. (1987). The role of the phoneme-to-grapheme conversion system and of the graphemic output buffer in writing: Evidence from an Italian case of pure dysgraphia. In M. Coltheart, G. Sartori, & R. Job (Eds.), *The cognitive neuropsychology of language.* Hove, UK: Lawrence Erlbaum Associates Ltd.

Miles, T.R. (1983). *Dyslexia: The pattern of difficulties.* London: Granada.

Mitterer, J.O. (1982). There are at least two kinds of poor readers: Whole-word poor readers and recoding poor readers. *Canadian Journal of Psychology, 36,* 445–461.

Monsell, S. (1985). Repetition and the lexicon. In A.W. Ellis (Ed.), *Progress in the psychology of language,* Vol. 2. Hove, UK: Lawrence Erlbaum Associates Ltd.

Monsell, S. (1991). The nature and locus of word frequency effects in reading. In D. Besner & G.W. Humphreys (Eds.), *Basic processes in reading: Visual word recognition.* Hillsdale, NJ: Lawrence Erlbaum Associates Inc.

Monsell, S., Doyle, M.C., & Haggard, P.N. (1989). Effects of frequency on visual word recognition tasks: Where are they? *Journal of Experimental Psychology: General, 118,* 43–71.

Moore, D.W. & Readence, J.E. (1980). A meta-analysis of the effects of graphic organisers on learning from text. In M.L. Kamil & A.J. Moe (Eds.), *Perspectives on reading research and instruction.* Washington, DC: National Reading Conference.

Morgan, P. (1896). A case of congenital word blindness. *British Medical Journal, 2,* 1378.

Morrison, C.M., Ellis, A.W., & Quinlan, P.T. (1992). Age of acquisition, not word frequency, affects object naming, not object recognition. *Memory and Cognition, 20,* 705–714.

Morton, J. (1964a). A preliminary functional model for language behaviour. *International Audiology, 3,* 216–225. Reprinted in R.C. Oldfield & J.C. Marshall (Eds.), *Language.* Harmondsworth: Penguin.

Morton, J. (1964b). A model for continuous language behaviour. *Language and Speech, 7,* 40–70.

Morton, J. (1969). Interaction of information in word recognition. *Psychological Review, 76,* 165–178.

Morton, J. (1979). Word recognition. In J. Morton & J.C. Marshall (Eds.), *Psycholinguistics Series,* Vol. 2. London: Elek.

Morton, J. (1980). The logogen model and orthographic structure. In U. Frith (Ed.), *Cognitive processes in spelling.* London: Academic Press.

Mozer, M.C. (1983). Letter migration and word perception. *Journal of Experimental Psychology: Human Perception and Performance, 9,* 531–546.

Naidoo, S. (1981). Teaching methods and their rationale. In G.Th. Pavlidis & T.R. Miles (Eds.), *Dyslexia research and its applications to education.* New York: John Wiley.

Neely, J.H. (1991). Semantic priming effects in visual word recognition: A selective review of current findings and theories. In D. Besner & G.W. Humphreys (Eds.), *Basic processes in reading: Visual word recognition.* Hillsdale, NJ: Lawrence Erlbaum Associates Inc.

Newcombe, F. & Marshall, J.C. (1980). Transcoding and lexical stabilization in deep dyslexia. In M. Coltheart, K.E. Patterson, & J.C. Marshall (Eds.), *Deep dyslexia.* London: Routledge and Kegan Paul.

Oakhill, J. (1983). Inferential and memory skills in children's comprehension of stories. *British Journal of Educational Psychology, 54,* 31–39.

Oakhill, J. & Garnham, A. (1988). *Becoming a skilled reader.* Oxford: Basil Blackwell.

Oakhill, J., Yuill, N., & Parkin, A.J. (1986). On the nature of the difference between skilled and less skilled comprehenders. *Journal of Research in Reading, 9,* 80–91.

Olson, R.K., Wise, B., Conners, F.A., & Rack, J.P. (1990). Specific deficits in component reading and language skills: Genetic and environmental influences. *Journal of Learning Disabilities, 22,* 339–348.

O'Regan, J.K. (1981). The convenient viewing position hypothesis. In D.F. Fisher, R.A. Monty, & J.W. Senders (Eds.), *Eye movements in reading: Cognition and visual perception.* Hillsdale, NJ: Lawrence Erlbaum Associates Inc.

Orton, S.T. (1931). Special disability in spelling. *Bulletin of the Neurological Clinic, 1,* 159–192.

Orton, S.T. (1937). *Reading, writing and speech problems in children.* New York: Norton.

Orton Dyslexia Society (1986). Some facts about illiteracy in America. *Perspectives on Dyslexia, 13,* 1–13.

Palincsar, A.S. & Brown, A.L. (1984). Reciprocal teaching of comprehension-fostering and comprehension-monitoring activities. *Cognition and Instruction, 1,* 117–175.

Palmer, J., MacLeod, C.M., Hunt, E., & Davidson, J. (1985). Information processing correlates of reading. *Journal of Memory and Language, 24,* 59–88.

Paris, S.G. & Oka, E.R. (1986). Children's reading strategies, metacognition and motivation. *Developmental Review, 6,* 25–56.

Parkin, A.J. (1982). Phonological recoding in lexical decision: Effects of spelling-to-sound regularity depend on how regularity is defined. *Memory and Cognition, 10,* 43–53.

Patterson, K.E. (1979). What's right with "deep" dyslexics? *Brain and Language, 8,* 111–129.

Patterson, K.E. (1982). The relation between reading and phonological coding: Further neuropsychological observations. In A.W. Ellis (Ed.), *Normality and pathology in cognitive functions.* London: Academic Press.

Patterson, K.E., & Coltheart, V. (1987). Phonological processes in reading: A tutorial review. In M. Coltheart (Ed.), *Attention and performance XII: The psychology of reading.* Hove, UK: Lawrence Erlbaum Associates Ltd.

Patterson, K.E. & Kay, J. (1982). Letter-by-letter reading: Psychological descriptions of a neurological syndrome. *Quarterly Journal of Experimental Psychology, 34A,* 411–441.

Patterson, K.E., Marshall, J.C., & Coltheart, M. (1985). *Surface dyslexia: Neuropsychological and cognitive studies of phonological reading.* Hove, UK: Lawrence Erlbaum Associates Ltd.

Patterson, K.E., Vargha-Khadem, F., & Polkey, C.E. (1989). Reading with one hemisphere. *Brain, 112,* 39–63.

Pearson, P.D. & Galagher, M. (1983). The instruction of reading comprehension. *Contemporary Educational Psychology, 8,* 317–344.

Perfetti, C.A. (1985). *Reading ability.* New York: Oxford University Press.

Perfetti, C.A. & Hogaboam, T. (1975). The relationship between single word decoding and reading comprehension skill. *Journal of Educational Psychology, 67,* 461–469.

Pillsbury, W.B. (1897). A study in apperception. *American Journal of Psychology, 8,* 315–393.

Pollatsek, A., Bolozky, S., Well, A.D., & Rayner, K. (1981). Asymmetries in the perceptual span for Israeli readers. *Brain and Language, 14,* 174–180.

Preston, K.A. (1935). The speed of word perception and its relation to reading ability. *Journal of General Psychology, 13,* 199–203.

Rack, J.P., Snowling, M.J., & Olson, R.K. (1992). The nonword reading deficit in developmental dyslexia: A review. *Reading Research Quarterly, 27,* 29–53.

Rayner, K. (1979). Eye guidance in reading: Fixation locations within words. *Perception, 8,* 21–30.

Rayner, K. & Duffy, S.A. (1986). Lexical complexity and fixation times in reading: Effects of word frequency, verb complexity, and lexical ambiguity. *Memory and Cognition, 14,* 191–201.

Rayner, K. & Pollatsek, A. (1989). *The psychology of reading.* Englewood Cliffs, NJ: Prentice-Hall.

Rayner, K., Well, A.D., & Pollatsek, A. (1980) Asymmetry of the effective visual field in reading. *Perception and Psychophysics, 27,* 537–544.

Read, C. (1971). Pre-school children's knowledge of English phonology. *Harvard Educational Review, 41,* 1–34.

Riddoch, M.J., Humphreys, G.W., Cleton, P., & Fery, P. (1991). Interaction of attentional and lexical processes in neglect dyslexia. *Cognitive Neuropsychology, 7,* 479–517.

Rumelhart, D.E. & Siple, P. (1974). Process of recognizing tachistoscopically presented words. *Psychological Review, 81,* 99–118.

Rumsey, J.M., Berman, K.F., Denckla, M.B., Hamburger, S.D., Kruesi, M.J., & Weinberger, D.R. (1987). Regional cerebral blood flow in severe developmental dyslexia. *Archives of Neurology, 44,* 1144–1150.

Sampson, G. (1985). *Writing systems.* London: Hutchinson.

Sanford, A.J. & Garrod, S.C. (1981). *Understanding written language.* Chichester: John Wiley.

Scarborough, D.L., Cortese, C., & Scarborough H.S. (1977). Frequency and repetition effects in lexical memory. *Journal of Experimental Psychology: Human Perception and Performance, 3,* 1–17.

Schank, R.C. (1982). *Dynamic memory.* Cambridge: Cambridge University Press.

Schank, R.C. & Abelson, R.P. (1977). *Scripts, plans, goals and understanding.* Hillsdale, NJ: Lawrence Erlbaum Associates Inc.

Schuberth, R.E. & Eimas, P. (1977). Effects of context on the classification of words and non-words. *Journal of Experimental Psychology: Human Perception and Performance, 3,* 27–36.

Schwartz, M.F., Marin, O.S.M., & Saffran, E.M. (1979). Dissociations of language function in dementia: A case study. *Brain and Language, 7,* 277–306.

Schwartz, M.F., Saffran, E.M., & Marin, O.S.M. (1980). Fractionating the reading process in dementia: Evidence for word-specific print-to-sound associations. In M. Coltheart, K.E. Patterson, & J.C. Marshall (Eds.), *Deep dyslexia*. London: Routledge and Kegan Paul.

Scragg, D.G. (1974). *A history of English spelling*. Manchester: Manchester University Press/New York: Barnes and Noble.

Seidenberg, M.S. & McClelland, J.L. (1989). A distributed, developmental model of word recognition and naming. *Psychological Review, 96*, 523–568.

Seidenberg, M.S., Waters, G.S., Barnes, M.A., & Tanenhaus, M.K. (1984). When does irregular spelling or pronunciation influence word recognition? *Journal of Verbal Learning and Verbal Behavior, 23*, 383–404.

Sejnowski, T.J. & Rosenberg, C.R. (1988). NETtalk: A parallel network that learns to read aloud. In J.A. Anderson & E. Rosenfeld (Eds.), *Neurocomputing*. Cambridge, MA.: MIT Press.

Seymour, P.H.K. (1986). *Cognitive analysis of dyslexia*. London: Routledge and Kegan Paul.

Seymour, P.H.K. (1987). Developmental dyslexia: A cognitive experimental analysis. In M. Coltheart, G. Sartori, & R. Job (Eds.), *The cognitive neuropsychology of language*. Hove, UK: Lawrence Erlbaum Associates Ltd.

Seymour, P.H.K. (1990). Developmental dyslexia. In M.W. Eysenck (Ed.), *Cognitive psychology: An international review*. Chichester: John Wiley.

Seymour, P.H.K. & Elder, L. (1986). Beginning reading without phonology. *Cognitive Neuropsychology, 3*, 1–36.

Seymour, P.H.K. & MacGregor, C.J. (1984). Developmental dyslexia: A cognitive developmental analysis of phonological, morphemic and visual impairments. *Cognitive Neuropsychology, 1*, 43–82.

Seymour, P.H.K. & Porpodas, C.D. (1980). Lexical and non-lexical processing of spelling in developmental dyslexia. In U. Frith (Ed.), *Cognitive processes in spelling*. London: Academic Press.

Shallice, T. (1981). Phonological agraphia and the lexical route in writing. *Brain, 104*, 413–429.

Shallice, T. (1988). *From neuropsychology to mental structure*. Cambridge: Cambridge University Press.

Shallice, T. & Warrington, E.K. (1977). The possible role of selective attention in acquired dyslexia. *Neuropsychologia, 15*, 31–41.

Shallice, T. & Warrington, E.K. (1980). Single and multiple component central dyslexic syndromes. In M. Coltheart, K.E. Patterson, & J.C. Marshall (Eds.), *Deep dyslexia*. London: Routledge and Kegan Paul.

Siegel, L.S. (1985). Deep dyslexia in childhood? *Brain and Language, 26*, 16–27.

Siegel, L.S. (1989). IQ is irrelevant to the definition of learning disabilities. *Journal of Learning Disabilities, 22*, 469–478.

Silberberg, N.E. & Silberberg, M.C. (1968). Case histories in hyperlexia. *Journal of School Psychology, 7*, 3–7.

Smiley, S.S., Oakley, D.D., Worthen, D., Campione, J.C., & Brown, A.L. (1977). Recall of thematically relevant material by adolescent good and poor readers as a function of written versus oral presentation. *Journal of Educational Psychology, 69*, 381–387.

Smith, E.E. & Collins, A.M. (1981). Use of goal-plan knowledge in understanding stories. In *Proceedings of the Third Annual Conference of the Cognitive Science Society*, Berkeley, CA, pp. 115–116.

Smyth, M.M. Morris, P.E., Levy, P., & Ellis, A.W. (1987). *Cognition in action.* Hove, UK: Lawrence Erlbaum Associates Ltd.

Snowling, M. (1980). The development of grapheme–phoneme correspondences in normal and dyslexic readers. *Journal of Experimental Child Psychology, 29,* 294–305.

Snowling, M. (1987). *Dyslexia: A cognitive developmental perspective.* Oxford: Basil Blackwell.

Snowling, M.J. (1991). Developmental reading disorders. *Journal of Child Psychology and Psychiatry, 32,* 49–77.

Snowling, M.J. & Hulme, C. (1989). A longitudinal case study of developmental phonological dyslexia. *Cognitive Neuropsychology, 6,* 379–401.

Snowling, M.J., Hulme, C., Wells, B., & Goulandris, N. (1992). Continuities between speech and spelling in a case of developmental dyslexia. *Reading and Writing: An Interdisciplinary Journal, 4,* 19–31.

Snowling, M.J., Stackhouse, J., & Rack, J.P. (1986). Phonological dyslexia and dysgraphia: A developmental analysis. *Cognitive Neuropsychology, 3,* 309–339.

Spring, C. & French, L. (1990). Identifying children with specific reading disabilities from listening and reading discrepancy scores. *Journal of Learning Disabilities, 23,* 53–58.

Stanovich, K.E. (1980). Toward an interactive-compensatory model of individual differences in the development of reading fluency. *Reading Research Quarterly, 16,* 32–71.

Stanovich, K.E. (1981). Attentional and automatic context effects in reading. In A.M. Lesgold & C. Perfetti (Eds.), *Interactive processes in reading.* Hillsdale, NJ: Lawrence Erlbaum Associates Inc.

Stanovich, K.E. (1991). Discrepancy definitions of reading disability: Has intelligence led us astray? *Reading Research Quarterly, 26,* 7–29.

Stanovich, K.E. & West, R.F. (1979). Mechanisms of sentence context effects in reading: Automatic activation and conscious attention. *Memory and Cognition, 7,* 77–85.

Stanovich, K.E. & West, R.F. (1983). On priming by a sentence context. *Journal of Experimental Psychology: General, 112,* 1–36.

Stanovich, K.E., Cunningham, A.E., & Cramer, B.B. (1984). Assessing phonological awareness in kindergarten children: Issues of task comparability. *Journal of Experimental Child Psychology, 38,* 175–190.

Stanovich, K.E., Cunningham, A.E., & Freeman, D.J. (1984). Intelligence, cognitive skills, and early reading progress. *Reading Research Quarterly, 19,* 278–303.

Stothard, S.E. (1992). *Reading difficulties in children: Problems of decoding and comprehension.* Unpublished DPhil thesis, University of York.

Stuart, M. & Coltheart, M. (1988). Does reading develop in a sequence of stages? *Cognition, 30,* 139–181.

Stuart, M. & Masterson, J. (1992). Patterns of reading and spelling in 10-year-old children related to prereading phonological abilities. *Journal of Experimental Child Psychology, 54,* 168–187.

Sulin, R.A. & Dooling, D.J. (1974). Intrusion of a thematic idea in retention of prose. *Journal of Experimental Psychology, 103,* 255–262.

Taraban, R. & McClelland, J.L. (1987). Conspiracy effects in word pronunciation. *Journal of Memory and Language, 25,* 608–631.

Temple, C. (1986). Developmental dysgraphias. *Quarterly Journal of Experimental Psychology, 38A,* 77–110.

Temple, C. & Marshall, J.C. (1983). A case study of developmental phonological dyslexia. *British Journal of Psychology, 74,* 517–533.

Thomson, M.E. (1988). Preliminary findings concerning the effects of specialised teaching on dyslexic children. *Applied Cognitive Psychology, 2,* 19–31.

Treiman, R. (1984). Individual differences between children in reading and spelling styles. *Journal of Experimental Child Psychology, 37,* 463–477.

Treiman, R. & Hirsh-Pasek, K. (1985). Are there qualitative differences in reading behaviour between dyslexics and normal readers? *Memory and Cognition, 13,* 357–364.

Tulving, E. & Gold, C. (1963). Stimulus information and contextual information as determinants of tachistoscopic recognition of words. *Journal of Experimental Psychology, 66,* 319–327.

Tunmer, W.E., Herriman, M.L., & Nesdale, A.R. (1988). Metalinguistic abilities and beginning reading. *Reading Research Quarterly, 23,* 134–158.

Van Dijk, T.A. & Kintsch, W. (1983). *Strategies of discourse comprehension.* New York: Academic Press.

Van Galen, G.P. (1991). Handwriting: Issues for a psychomotor theory. *Human Movement Science, 10,* 165–191.

Van Orden, G.C. (1987). A rows is a rose: Spelling, sound, and reading. *Memory and Cognition, 15,* 181–198.

Van Orden, G.C., Johnston, J.C., & Hale, B.L. (1988). Word identification in reading proceeds from spelling to sound to meaning. *Journal of Experimental Psychology: Learning, Memory and Cognition, 14,* 371–386.

Van Orden, G.C., Pennington, B.F., & Stone, G.O. (1990). Word identification in reading and the promise of subsymbolic psycholinguistics. *Psychological Review, 97,* 488–522.

Venezky, R.L. (1980). From Webster to Rice to Roosevelt: The formative years for spelling instruction and spelling reform in the USA. In U. Frith (Ed.), *Cognitive processes in spelling.* London: Academic Press.

Vogler, G.P., DeFries, J.C., & Decker, S.N. (1985). Family history as an indicator of risk for reading disability. *Journal of Learning Disabilities, 18,* 419–421.

Wagner, R. & Torgeson, J. (1987). The nature of phonological processing and its causal role in the acquisition of reading skills. *Psychological Bulletin, 101,* 192–212.

Warren, C. & Morton, J. (1982). The effects of priming on picture recognition. *British Journal of Psychology, 73,* 117–130.

Warrington, E.K. & Shallice, T. (1980). Word-form dyslexia. *Brain, 103,* 99–112.

Wason, P.C. (1980). Specific thoughts on the writing process. In L.W. Gregg & E.R. Steinberg (Eds.), *Cognitive processes in writing.* Hillsdale, NJ: Lawrence Erlbaum Associates Inc.

Waters, G.S., Seidenberg, M.S., & Bruck, M. (1984). Children's and adults' use of spelling–sound information in three reading tasks. *Memory and Cognition, 12,* 293–305.

Wells, F.L. (1906). Linguistic lapses. In J.McK. Cattell & F.J.E. Woodbridge (Eds.), *Archives of Philosophy, Psychology and Scientific Methods No. 6.* New York: Science Press.

West, R.F. & Stanovich, K.E. (1978). Automatic contextual facilitation in readers of three ages. *Child Development, 49,* 717–727.

Wilding, J. (1989). Developmental dyslexics do not fit in boxes: Evidence from six new case studies. *European Journal of Cognitive Psychology, 1,* 105–127.

Wilding, J. (1990). Developmental dyslexics do not fit in boxes: Evidence from the case studies. *European Journal of Cognitive Psychology, 2,* 97–131.

Yuill, N. & Joscelyne, T. (1988). Effects of organisational cues and strategies on good and poor comprehenders' story understanding. *Journal of Educational Psychology, 2,* 152–158.

Yuill, N. & Oakhill, J. (1988). Effects of inference awareness training on poor reading comprehension. *Applied Cognitive Psychology, 2,* 33–45.

Yuill, N. & Oakhill, J. (1991). *Children's problems in text comprehension.* Cambridge: Cambridge University Press.

Zangwill, O.L. (1939). Some relations between reproducing and recognising prose material. *British Journal of Psychology, 29,* 371–382.

Author Index

Subject Index